All About Black Forest: A Kid's Guide to Germany's Famous Woodland

Educational Books For Kids, Volume 43

Shah Rukh

Published by Shah Rukh, 2024.

While every precaution has been taken in the preparation of this book, the publisher assumes no responsibility for errors or omissions, or for damages resulting from the use of the information contained herein.

ALL ABOUT BLACK FOREST: A KID'S GUIDE TO GERMANY'S FAMOUS WOODLAND

First edition. November 6, 2024.

Copyright © 2024 Shah Rukh.

ISBN: 979-8227806345

Written by Shah Rukh.

Table of Contents

Prologue 1
Chapter 1: Legends of the Black Forest 2
Chapter 2: The Wild Animals That Call It Home 5
Chapter 3: Tales of Hidden Treasure 9
Chapter 4: The Mysterious Cuckoo Clocks 13
Chapter 5: Hiking Trails for Young Explorers 17
Chapter 6: Magical Plants and Enchanted Trees 21
Chapter 7: The Oldest Castles in the Forest 26
Chapter 8: Discovering Waterfalls and Lakes 31
Chapter 9: Stories of Forest Fairies and Spirits 36
Chapter 10: Black Forest Cakes and Sweet Treats 41
Chapter 11: How the Forest Changes Through the Seasons 46
Chapter 12: Meet the People Who Live in the Forest Villages 50
Chapter 13: Secret Caves and Underground Wonders 55
Chapter 14: Ancient Myths and Famous Folktales 60
Chapter 15: Animals That Only Come Out at Night 65
Chapter 16: Forest Music and Traditional Songs 70
Chapter 17: Exploring the Black Forest by Bike 74
Chapter 18: The Forest's Biggest Festivals and Celebrations 79
Chapter 19: Black Forest Adventures in Winter 83
Chapter 20: Protecting the Forest and Its Future 87
Epilogue 92

Prologue

Welcome, young adventurers! Have you ever wondered what it would be like to step into a place where fairy tales come to life, where the trees are so tall they seem to touch the sky, and where mysteries wait around every corner? If you have, then you're about to embark on an incredible journey into the heart of one of the most magical places on Earth—the Black Forest.

Nestled in southwestern Germany, the Black Forest is more than just a woodland; it's a world full of stories, secrets, and surprises. This forest has inspired countless legends about cunning dwarfs, helpful fairies, and enchanted creatures. But it's not just the tales that make the Black Forest special; it's the wildlife that roams freely, the rushing rivers, the towering mountains, and the peaceful villages that have called it home for centuries.

In this book, we'll uncover everything that makes the Black Forest famous. From its history and wildlife to its fun activities and tasty treats, you'll find out what makes this forest one of a kind. We'll learn about the people who live there, the traditions they celebrate, and the breathtaking sights you can see if you ever visit.

So, put on your explorer's hat, grab your flashlight, and get ready to step into a forest full of wonder. The Black Forest is calling—let's find out what adventures await!

Chapter 1: Legends of the Black Forest

The Black Forest is not just a place filled with trees, birds, and beautiful scenery. It is a magical land full of stories that have been told for hundreds of years. Imagine a forest so thick and mysterious that people long ago believed all sorts of strange creatures lived there. The towering trees, deep shadows, and whispering winds made it the perfect place for stories to come alive. The Black Forest is famous for its legends that include brave knights, cunning witches, helpful fairies, and even dragons that guarded hidden treasures.

One of the most popular legends from the Black Forest is that of the *Erdmannleins*, who are tiny, gnome-like creatures said to live deep underground. These little folk are known for being clever miners and skilled at finding shiny gems and precious metals. People believed that if you treated the Erdmannleins kindly and respected the forest, they might help you by showing you where to find gold or by giving you advice. But if you were greedy or mean, they would trick you and make you lose your way in the forest until you were completely confused!

There are also tales of witches who lived in hidden cottages far off the main paths. They were said to cast spells and brew strange potions. While some stories describe them as wicked and scary, others tell of wise women who could heal the sick and knew the secrets of the plants in the forest. People who dared to enter the deep woods would sometimes come across strange signs carved into tree trunks or little bundles of twigs tied together, clues that they were near a witch's home. Many children would listen wide-eyed as their parents told them never to stray too far into the woods, just in case they stumbled upon one of these mysterious women.

The Black Forest is also known for tales of powerful and mighty giants. According to some stories, these giants used the mountains and hills as their playground. They could lift huge boulders and build castles in the blink of an eye. Some of the old castles and ruins you can still see today are said to be left behind by these giants. People whispered that at night, if you listened carefully, you could hear the echo of their booming voices in the distance as they called out to one another across the valleys.

Another famous legend is about a creature called the *Höllentäler*, which is said to roam the thickest, darkest parts of the Black Forest. This beast had glowing red eyes and a howl that could freeze anyone who heard it in their tracks. Villagers would tell stories of travelers who dared to walk through the forest at night only to hear the creature's eerie cry. Some believed the Höllentäler protected the forest and only scared away those who wanted to harm it. While people who took care of the forest were safe, those with bad intentions would be chased away, never to be seen again.

There are even tales of enchanted lakes and rivers hidden deep in the forest. One story is about the *Mummelsee*, a lake that people say is home to water spirits known as *Nixes*. These beautiful spirits with flowing hair and sparkling eyes would sometimes come out at night to dance on the water's surface. But if a person tried to approach them, they would vanish in a splash of water, disappearing beneath the waves. Some believed that if you left a gift like a flower or a pretty stone by the lake, the Nixes might bring you good luck or help you with a wish.

One of the most exciting legends is about a hero named Hans, who was said to have defeated a fearsome dragon that lived in a cave near the edge of the Black Forest. According to the tale, Hans was just a young man with a brave heart. He took on the challenge to protect his village when he heard the dragon was stealing sheep and scaring everyone. With only a simple sword and his courage, Hans fought the dragon until he managed to outsmart it and send it fleeing into the mountains. The villagers celebrated him as a hero and claimed that on stormy nights, you could still hear the roar of the dragon as it sulked in its distant cave.

Of course, no collection of Black Forest legends would be complete without mentioning the stories of magical clocks. The Black Forest is where the famous cuckoo clock was invented, and people believed that some clocks had a little bit of magic in them. There were stories of clocks that could tell the future or warn their owners of danger with an extra loud "cuckoo!" or even stop ticking when something mysterious was about to happen. Imagine living in a cottage surrounded by forest, where your clock isn't just a timepiece but a friend with a few tricks up its sleeve!

These tales were not just for fun; they were a way for people to teach important lessons. Many stories encouraged children to be brave, kind, and respectful of nature. They reminded everyone that the forest was full of wonder and mystery and that those who walked through it should do so carefully and with an open heart. The Black Forest may be a real place, but its legends make it feel like something out of a fairy tale, where anything is possible, and the line between reality and magic is as thin as the mist that creeps through the trees at dawn.

Chapter 2: The Wild Animals That Call It Home

The Black Forest is more than just a place with trees and ancient legends; it's a living, breathing home to a wide variety of wild animals that make the forest feel full of life. When you walk through the winding trails, you might not see them all at once, but they're there, hidden in the leaves, darting through the underbrush, or gliding through the sky. Each animal plays its own role in keeping the forest alive and balanced, and each has its own story to tell.

One of the most famous animals in the Black Forest is the red deer. These magnificent creatures are the kings and queens of the forest, with their strong antlers and sleek brown fur. In the early morning or at dusk, you might catch a glimpse of a stag standing proudly, listening carefully to the sounds of the forest. During the fall, the forest echoes with the deep, powerful calls of the stags, a sound that's called "the rut." This is when the males show off and challenge each other for the attention of the females. It's a sight and sound that reminds everyone that the forest is wild and full of life.

Another animal that calls the Black Forest home is the shy and clever fox. With its bright, bushy tail and sharp eyes, the fox sneaks around the forest, looking for small creatures like mice, rabbits, and birds. Foxes are known for being smart and quick on their feet, and they can hide so well that you might pass by one without even knowing it was there. People who live near the forest often tell stories of seeing a flash of red fur or hearing the soft patter of paws on the forest floor when the sun begins to set.

The Black Forest is also home to many wild boars, which are like forest pigs but bigger and much tougher. These animals travel in groups called sounders and use their strong snouts to dig up roots and plants. If you're walking in the forest and see patches of earth that look like they've been turned over, it's probably the work of a wild boar. They might look scary with their sharp tusks, but they're usually more interested in finding food than in bothering people. However, if you ever come across one, it's best to stay back and watch from a distance.

High up in the treetops, you might hear the calls of many types of birds. The Black Forest is famous for its birds, especially the woodpeckers that tap-tap-tap on the trees. The sound of a woodpecker is like the forest's own music. These birds use their strong beaks to peck at the wood to find insects to eat or to make a hole for their nests. If you're lucky, you might even spot the great spotted woodpecker with its red, black, and white feathers, or the rare black woodpecker, which is much larger and has a shiny black body with a striking red crown.

Owls are another special bird you might encounter. The most famous owl in the Black Forest is the tawny owl, which makes a "hoo-hoo" sound that is both spooky and magical, especially at night. These owls are expert hunters and have amazing night vision, which helps them find mice and other small creatures even in the darkest parts of the forest. When you hear an owl's call echo through the trees at night, it feels like the forest is talking to you, sharing its secrets.

Squirrels also make their home in the Black Forest, and they're some of the most playful and fun animals to watch. The squirrels in the Black Forest are usually red with fluffy tails, and they dart from branch to branch with amazing speed. You might see one stop to nibble on an acorn or hide a nut in the ground to save for later. These little creatures are always busy, and they help the forest by spreading seeds, which helps new plants grow.

The forest floor is home to many other creatures, too, like hedgehogs and badgers. Hedgehogs are small, spiky animals that curl up into a ball when they're scared. They like to come out in the evening and search for insects and worms to snack on. Badgers, on the other hand, are tougher and live in burrows that they dig with their strong claws. They are mostly active at night and are known for being very clean animals, often sweeping out their burrows to keep them nice and tidy.

The Black Forest is also known for having some predators, like the lynx. The lynx is a big, wild cat with tufted ears and a short tail. It moves silently through the forest and is rarely seen because it's so good at blending in with its surroundings. The lynx used to be almost gone from the Black Forest, but thanks to efforts to protect wildlife, it has been making a comeback. It's a true symbol of the wildness of the forest, reminding people that even though it's beautiful, it's also untamed and full of surprises.

Among the smaller animals, there are many kinds of frogs and lizards that live in the damp, mossy parts of the forest. These tiny creatures might not be as big or as loud as the deer or the boars, but they are just as important. Frogs sing their croaky songs in the spring, while lizards sunbathe on rocks during warmer days. They are part of the forest's natural orchestra, adding their sounds to the chorus of birds and the rustling of leaves.

In the rivers and streams that run through the Black Forest, fish like trout swim through the cool, clear water. Sometimes, if you sit quietly by a stream, you might even spot an otter playing in the water or searching for its next meal. Otters are fun to watch because they slide and tumble around, enjoying the water as if it's their playground. They are also a sign that the water in the forest is clean and healthy, which is very important for all the animals living there.

Bees, butterflies, and beetles are everywhere in the Black Forest, buzzing and fluttering from flower to flower. These insects are more than just pretty to look at; they help pollinate plants, which means they help flowers and trees grow. Without them, the forest would not be as lush and full of life. You can often see bright blue butterflies or beetles with shiny, colorful shells. They add to the magical feeling of the forest, making it seem like it's sprinkled with tiny pieces of living art.

The Black Forest is a special place because of all the creatures that live there. Each animal, big or small, has a role that keeps the forest healthy and thriving. From the quiet deer standing in the morning mist to the owl calling through the night, the forest is full of stories waiting to be discovered. It's a reminder that the world is full of wonders, and that nature is always at work, even when we don't see it.

Chapter 3: Tales of Hidden Treasure

The Black Forest is not just famous for its towering trees and deep, shadowy trails; it's also known as a place where many believe hidden treasures lie buried, waiting to be discovered. For hundreds of years, stories have been passed down through families and communities about lost riches, secret stashes of gold, and hidden jewels hidden deep within the forest's heart. These tales of hidden treasure make the forest feel even more mysterious, as if each rock and tree might be guarding a long-forgotten secret.

One of the most well-known stories is about the *Treasure of the Count*. According to legend, there was once a powerful count who ruled over the region around the Black Forest. He was known for being both rich and cautious, always afraid that his enemies would steal his wealth. To protect his treasure, he ordered his most trusted men to hide it somewhere safe within the forest. They carried bags of gold, silver, and precious gems deep into the woods, finding a hidden cave behind a waterfall to stash the riches. They created an elaborate set of traps and puzzles to ensure that only someone very clever or lucky could ever find it. Some say that if you listen carefully when you stand near certain waterfalls, you can hear the faint clinking of gold coins or the whispers of the count's men as they made their secret plans.

Another famous tale is about the *Lost Crown of the Woodland King*. Long ago, it's said that a king who loved the forest more than anything else in his kingdom crafted a beautiful crown made entirely of emeralds and rare forest stones. This king was wise and gentle, and he ruled alongside the creatures of the Black Forest, treating them as friends. When the king grew old and knew his time was nearing its end, he hid the crown somewhere in the forest as a gift to the land that had given him so much joy. He left behind a riddle that only the bravest and kindest of heart could solve. The riddle hinted at a place where the shadows meet the sun, where an ancient tree cradles a hidden nest, and where the forest sings with the sound of birds in the early morning. Treasure hunters have searched for generations, but no one has found the crown yet, and some believe that it still lies hidden, waiting for the right person to discover it.

There are also many stories about the *Gold Miners' Fortune*. During the 16th and 17th centuries, people flocked to the Black Forest to try their luck at finding gold. Small mining towns popped up, and there were whispers of miners who struck it rich and quickly vanished, fearing that someone might steal their newfound wealth. According to one story, a group of miners who discovered a particularly large vein of gold decided to bury their riches in the forest for safekeeping. They planned to return for it once they could leave the area safely. Unfortunately, before they could come back, a fierce storm hit the forest, and they lost their way in the confusion. Some versions of the tale say that the miners were never seen again, while others claim they returned years later, only to find that the forest had changed and they could no longer remember where the treasure was hidden. Today, treasure hunters still search for clues, hoping to stumble upon an old map or find a hint of where the Gold Miners' Fortune lies.

The Black Forest is also home to stories about hidden treasure guarded by mystical beings. One popular tale is about the *Treasure of the Erdmannleins*, the small, gnome-like creatures who live underground and are said to be skilled at finding and hiding precious metals. The story goes that these tiny miners discovered a huge collection of gold and jewels beneath the forest floor. But instead of keeping it for themselves, they decided to store it in a secret chamber that only they knew about. The Erdmannleins were friendly to those who respected the forest, and some people say that if you show kindness to the animals and plants in the forest, the Erdmannleins might leave small gifts of shiny stones or lead you to a hidden piece of their treasure.

Then there's the tale of *The Cursed Silver*, which tells of a group of bandits who once roamed the forest. These bandits were notorious for stealing from travelers who passed through the forest. They gathered a massive pile of silver coins and other stolen items and hid them in a cave deep in the woods. But the bandits were not kind to the forest or its creatures, and according to legend, an old woman who was said to be a forest witch put a curse on them. She warned that their treasure would bring bad luck to anyone who tried to take it. The bandits laughed and ignored her warning, but strange things began to happen. They quarreled among themselves, and soon, they vanished without a trace. The cave where the treasure was hidden is said to be protected by the witch's curse, and those who search for it claim to hear whispers and feel a cold chill, as if unseen eyes are watching them.

One of the most exciting legends is about *The Treasure Map of the Black Knight*. In the days when knights and castles were a common sight, there was a knight known as the Black Knight, who was said to be as mysterious as the forest itself. He wore dark armor and traveled alone, protecting the hidden trails and keeping watch over secret paths that few knew about. Some believed he was guarding a legendary treasure, one so valuable that kings would have sent entire armies to claim it. Before the Black Knight disappeared, he supposedly left behind a map carved into the wood of a tree, a map that could only be read under the light of the full moon. Treasure hunters have searched for this tree for hundreds of years, hoping to find the map that will lead them to the knight's fabled hoard.

There is also the story of *The Fairy's Gold*, which speaks of a tiny but powerful fairy queen who had a collection of golden leaves that glittered brighter than the sun. These leaves were said to be so magical that they could bring good fortune to anyone who found them. But the fairy queen was wise and knew that not everyone deserved such luck, so she hid the golden leaves in a place surrounded by tricky paths and guarded by creatures that could shape-shift to look like rocks or trees.

If someone with a pure heart wandered near, the forest might reveal a glimmer of gold to them. But for those driven by greed, the forest would close around them, leading them in circles until they gave up and went home empty-handed.

Every tale of hidden treasure in the Black Forest is wrapped in mystery and adventure. It's said that the forest itself knows where the treasures are hidden and decides who is worthy of finding them. Whether it's the quiet rustle of leaves in the wind, the distant hoot of an owl, or the faint sound of a stream trickling over rocks, every sound in the Black Forest could be a hint. People who explore the forest today still wonder if they might be the lucky one to find a hidden chest of gold, a glittering jewel, or a map carved by a long-lost knight. These tales remind us that the forest is not just a place of natural beauty but a realm of imagination and endless possibilities.

Chapter 4: The Mysterious Cuckoo Clocks

The Black Forest isn't just famous for its tall, dark trees, winding trails, and hidden treasures—it's also the birthplace of one of the world's most charming and mysterious inventions: the cuckoo clock. These delightful clocks aren't just regular timekeepers; they are works of art that have fascinated people for centuries. The story of the cuckoo clock is filled with creativity, skill, and a touch of mystery, making them one of the most recognizable symbols of the Black Forest.

The tale of the cuckoo clock begins a long time ago in the 17th century, when craftsmen in the Black Forest region were looking for ways to earn a living during the harsh winter months when farming and other outdoor work were impossible. These artisans were skilled in woodworking and had a keen eye for detail. They used their talents to carve beautiful items out of wood, such as toys, tools, and, eventually, clocks. The clocks they made were not like the plain ones you see today; they were decorated with intricate carvings of animals, trees, flowers, and scenes from the forest itself. This was the perfect way for the people to showcase their love for the forest that surrounded them.

One day, someone had the brilliant idea to make a clock that had a little bird pop out to announce the time. This bird would call out a sound similar to its own call—"cuckoo!"—which is how the cuckoo clock got its name. The idea caught on quickly, and soon, workshops all over the Black Forest were making cuckoo clocks with their own unique twists. Some of these clocks featured not only a cuckoo bird but also other moving parts, like tiny woodcutters, dancing couples, and even miniature animals that moved in time with the clock's chime. Each clock was a little story on its own, bringing a piece of the forest into people's homes.

The cuckoo itself became a mysterious symbol. People in the Black Forest believed that the cuckoo bird was not just a regular bird but a magical creature that could bring good luck and predict the future. Some legends even said that if you heard the first call of the cuckoo in spring, you should turn over any coins in your pocket to make sure you would have good fortune all year long. Because of these beliefs, owning a cuckoo clock was seen as more than just having a timekeeper; it was like having a little guardian from the forest right on your wall.

Making a cuckoo clock was, and still is, a very special process. The clockmakers would carefully select pieces of wood, often using linden or pinewood, which are common in the Black Forest. They would carve the wood into detailed scenes, often showing nature, animals, and stories from their folklore. It was not uncommon for a single clock to take weeks or even months to complete because of the delicate work that went into carving the figures and making sure all the gears and pieces worked perfectly together. Each clock was painted by hand, with bright colors that made the little figures and details come to life.

The heart of every cuckoo clock is the mechanism that makes the cuckoo bird pop out and call. Inside the clock, there are tiny bellows and pipes that create the "cuckoo" sound. These parts have to be just the right size and shape, or the call won't sound right. This is why people say that making a perfect cuckoo clock requires not just skill but a little bit of magic as well. In the past, it was said that some clockmakers would work in secret, hiding their methods from others to make sure their clocks were the best and most unique.

There are stories about clocks that seemed to have a life of their own. One legend tells of an old clockmaker named Wilhelm who was known for making the most beautiful and accurate cuckoo clocks in the entire Black Forest. People came from far and wide to buy his clocks, which were said to never miss a beat. But Wilhelm was very private and mysterious, working late into the night by candlelight. Some people said they saw strange lights flickering in his workshop, and others claimed they heard whispers and the faint sound of laughter coming from within. According to the legend, Wilhelm's best clocks were blessed by the fairies of the forest, who helped him craft the tiniest, most perfect details. After Wilhelm passed away, some of his clocks were found to stop ticking at odd times, only to start again as if they had a mind of their own.

There is another tale of a village where a clock was said to have magical powers. This cuckoo clock hung in the main hall of a small inn and was known for chiming at exactly the right time, even when its gears were broken. The innkeeper, Frau Lena, said the clock was a gift from her grandfather, who claimed he had found it after a mysterious walk in the forest. The story goes that one stormy night, when a group of travelers was stuck at the inn due to bad weather, the clock began to chime all by itself, even though it hadn't been wound in weeks. With each chime, the storm outside lessened until it finally stopped, and the skies cleared. From that day on, the clock was treated as a special guardian of the inn, and no one dared move it or try to fix it for fear of losing its magic.

Even today, the Black Forest's cuckoo clocks hold a certain mystique. Modern clockmakers use many of the same methods their ancestors did, carving wood by hand and assembling each tiny piece with great care. Some clocks are simple, showing only the cuckoo bird and a little house, while others are grand and elaborate, featuring scenes with dancing figures, hunters, and even tiny musicians that play as the clock chimes. Many of these clocks are designed to tell stories, just like the legends of the forest they come from.

Owning a cuckoo clock is still seen as having a piece of the Black Forest right in your home. People love to listen for the cheerful "cuckoo" call, which seems to bring a bit of the outdoors inside. Some people believe that having a cuckoo clock brings good energy and that its calls fill the house with joy. Others are simply amazed at the skill and creativity that go into making these tiny works of art.

And while many clocks today are made with modern tools, the most special ones are still those made in small workshops by master craftsmen. These artisans keep the spirit of the forest alive with each piece they create, passing down their skills and secrets to younger generations. Walking into one of these workshops feels like stepping into another world, where time moves at its own pace, and the walls are filled with the ticking and tocking of clocks in every shape and size.

Some people who visit the Black Forest say that when they hear the cuckoo call for the first time, they feel as though they are part of a story, just like the ones told about hidden treasures and magical creatures. Whether it's the simple joy of seeing the little bird pop out or the thought of the ancient legends behind them, cuckoo clocks are more than just timepieces—they are a bridge to a world of wonder, where the past whispers secrets and the forest's mysteries are just a tick and a tock away.

Chapter 5: Hiking Trails for Young Explorers

The Black Forest is an incredible place for anyone who loves to explore the outdoors, and for young adventurers, it's like stepping into a world where stories come to life. Hiking through this magical forest is one of the best ways to discover all its wonders, from towering trees that touch the sky to sparkling streams that seem to sing as they flow. The forest is crisscrossed with trails that are perfect for young explorers who are ready for an adventure, each one with its own surprises and stories waiting to be uncovered.

One of the most exciting trails for young hikers is the *Witches' Path*, or *Hexenpfad*, a trail that feels like it's straight out of a fairy tale. This path is filled with twists and turns that wind through thick, dark woods where sunlight peeks through the branches, casting playful shadows on the ground. Along the way, kids can spot hidden carvings of witches and other magical creatures peeking out from behind trees or tucked into little nooks. Some parts of the trail are lined with wooden sculptures of gnomes, witches, and woodland animals, which add a touch of whimsy and make it feel like you're walking through an enchanted forest. The trail is safe and not too difficult, so even younger hikers can enjoy it without getting too tired. As you hike, you might hear the rustle of leaves and imagine it's the whisper of a witch or the chatter of friendly forest gnomes.

Another great path for young explorers is the *Lake Mummelsee Trail*. Mummelsee is a mysterious, shimmering lake surrounded by trees that seem to lean over it as if they're guarding a secret. According to old legends, the lake is home to a water spirit called the *Mummelsee King*, who lives beneath the surface with his family. The trail around the lake is easy to walk and perfect for kids who like to keep an eye out for clues that the water spirit might be nearby. Maybe you'll spot a ripple that seems to move on its own or hear the soft plop of a fish jumping out of the water. The air around the lake is cool and fresh, and on a quiet day, you might even hear the gentle sound of a breeze whispering through the reeds. There are also places where families can stop to rest, have a picnic, and enjoy the view of the sparkling water and surrounding mountains.

For those who love a bit of mystery, the *Trail of the Lost Castle* is a must. This path leads young explorers through dense woods and over gentle hills, eventually arriving at the ruins of an old stone castle. Although the castle has been worn down by time, its crumbling walls and moss-covered stones make it easy to imagine knights and princesses who might have once lived there. Kids can climb over the stones, peer through the broken windows, and imagine that they're brave adventurers searching for a hidden treasure. The trail to the castle isn't very steep, making it great for kids, and the forest around it is full of wildlife like squirrels, birds, and even the occasional deer peeking out from behind the trees.

For those who enjoy learning about nature as they explore, the *Nature Discovery Trail* is perfect. This trail is designed especially for young hikers and families, with signs along the way that teach about the different plants and animals found in the Black Forest. Each sign has fun facts and pictures, so kids can learn things like which trees grow the tallest, what kinds of birds sing in the branches, and how the forest animals make their homes. The trail is dotted with wooden bridges, small clearings, and cozy spots to sit and rest. Some parts of the path even have little challenges, like balance beams made from logs and stepping stones across shallow streams, which make the hike feel like an obstacle course designed by nature itself.

If you're looking for something a bit more magical, the *Fairy Tale Trail* is a journey that brings stories to life. This trail is lined with sculptures and scenes from famous fairy tales like *Hansel and Gretel* and *Little Red Riding Hood*. Kids can pause at each spot to listen to the story or read a sign that explains what part of the tale they're looking at. Some sculptures move or make sounds, like a wolf that howls or a witch's cauldron that bubbles, making the trail feel interactive and fun. The forest along this path feels alive with stories, and it's easy to imagine that a talking animal or a fairy might pop out to join you on your walk. It's a perfect trail for sparking the imagination and making kids feel like they've stepped into a storybook.

One of the most breathtaking trails for young hikers is the *Panorama Path*. This trail winds up a gentle slope that leads to a viewpoint overlooking the vast, green expanse of the Black Forest. The climb is not too steep, so kids can make their way up without much trouble, and there are plenty of places to stop and rest along the way. When you reach the top, the view is unforgettable. You can see treetops stretching as far as the eye can see, with rolling hills and the occasional glimmer of a hidden lake or the rooftops of a distant village. It's a great spot to take pictures, share a snack, and soak in the wonder of the forest from above. On clear days, you can even spot the distant peaks of the Alps, which makes the hike feel like an adventure that stretches across the world.

For families who enjoy a bit of a challenge, the *Adventure Trail of Giants* offers a fun and educational experience. This trail is known for its giant wooden statues that are scattered along the path. These statues include huge wooden carvings of animals like bears and eagles, as well as mythical creatures from Black Forest legends. Kids can stand next to these giant figures and feel as if they've shrunk down to the size of a mouse or that they've entered a world where animals rule the forest. Some parts of the trail have puzzles to solve or scavenger hunts to complete, which adds to the sense of adventure. The trail weaves through old trees with twisted roots and ferns that grow taller than most kids, giving the feeling of being in a forest that's full of ancient secrets.

One of the more mysterious and fun trails is the *Echo Valley Path*. This trail leads to a part of the forest where sound travels in a strange way, creating echoes that make your voice bounce back to you. Kids love stopping here to shout and hear their own voices repeated by the forest. It feels like the trees themselves are talking back, adding to the magical experience of the hike. The trail is shaded by tall pines, making it a cool, refreshing walk even on warmer days. Along the way, you might see tiny wildflowers growing in patches of sunlight, adding a splash of color to the green and brown forest floor.

The Black Forest also offers the *Tree Top Walk*, which is perfect for young explorers who aren't afraid of heights. This trail takes you on a wooden bridge that rises up into the treetops, where you can walk among the branches and see the forest from a bird's-eye view. There are platforms where you can stop to look out over the sea of green and learn about the different layers of the forest, from the mossy floor to the sunlit canopy above. The Tree Top Walk is not just fun—it's educational, teaching kids about how trees grow, the animals that live in the upper parts of the forest, and how everything in the forest is connected. At the highest point, there's usually a lookout tower where kids can climb even higher for a 360-degree view that makes them feel like they're on top of the world.

Each of these trails offers something different, from stories and legends to nature lessons and breathtaking views. For young explorers, hiking in the Black Forest is like going on a series of mini-adventures, where each step brings a new surprise. Whether you're searching for signs of the Mummelsee King, listening for echoes in the woods, or climbing up to see the world from the treetops, the forest is full of wonders that make every hike unforgettable. With each trail, kids learn to appreciate nature, discover the magic of the outdoors, and create memories that will last a lifetime.

Chapter 6: Magical Plants and Enchanted Trees

The Black Forest is not only famous for its dark, dense woods and fairy tale legends, but it is also a place where nature itself seems to hold a touch of magic. This enchanted forest is filled with plants and trees that have stories woven into their leaves, bark, and roots. For young explorers who step into the Black Forest, learning about the magical plants and enchanted trees that call this place home can feel like stepping into a world of myths and wonders.

One of the most legendary trees in the Black Forest is the *Elder Tree*. This tree, with its twisted branches and clusters of small white flowers, has been part of stories and folklore for centuries. People in the old days believed that the elder tree was the home of a wise, protective spirit. According to legends, if you were kind to the tree, it would bring you good fortune and guard your home from evil. But if you tried to cut it down or harm it without permission, bad luck was sure to follow. The elder tree was said to whisper secrets to those who sat beneath its branches and listened closely, and its berries and flowers were believed to have magical healing properties. Even today, people still use elderberries to make syrup and tea that is said to help with colds and boost the immune system. It's easy to imagine that, with its strong connection to healing, the elder tree might really have a touch of magic hidden in its roots.

Another plant with an air of mystery is *Moss*, which covers the forest floor and climbs up tree trunks like a soft, green blanket. In the Black Forest, moss isn't just decoration—it's a sign of the forest's age and wisdom. Stories tell of ancient travelers who found their way home by following the moss, which always grows thicker on the north side of trees. Some old tales say that fairies use the moss as their carpets, and at night, under the silver moonlight, you might even see them dancing.

The moss in the Black Forest adds to the feeling that you've stepped into another world, one where nature holds secrets that only those who believe in magic can discover.

The towering *Beech Trees* are also an important part of the forest's enchantment. These trees have smooth, silver-gray bark and leaves that turn a bright, golden color in the fall. Beech trees were once believed to be wise protectors that kept watch over the forest. It was said that if you leaned your ear against a beech tree and listened carefully, you could hear the stories of the forest—tales of animals, long-lost travelers, and ancient creatures that lived deep within the woods. Some stories tell of how the beech trees could move their branches to point people in the right direction if they were lost or protect them from harm by blocking paths with their roots. The leaves of the beech tree were also considered special. In olden days, people believed that writing a wish on a beech leaf and letting it fly away in the wind would make the wish come true.

A truly magical plant found in the Black Forest is the *Wolfsbane*, also known as *Monkshood* because of the shape of its dark purple flowers. Wolfsbane is famous in folklore for being a plant with both protective and dangerous powers. It was believed to ward off werewolves and witches, which is why people in medieval times would hang it above their doors or plant it around their homes for protection. However, the plant is also very poisonous, which added to its reputation as something powerful and not to be trifled with. Legends told that witches would use wolfsbane in their potions to make them stronger or to cast spells that could control wolves. Its mysterious nature makes it one of the more intriguing plants in the forest, surrounded by both fear and fascination.

The *Oak Tree* is another giant of the Black Forest that holds a special place in stories and myths. Oaks are known for their strength and longevity, and they were often thought to be trees of great wisdom. Druids, who were ancient priests and wise men, would gather in sacred groves of oak trees to perform their ceremonies, believing that these trees were a bridge between the earth and the spirit world. The acorns of the oak tree were considered lucky charms, symbols of strength, and were said to bring good luck to anyone who carried one in their pocket. Some even believed that the oak trees could grant protection to those who asked for it in times of need. When the wind rustles through the leaves of an oak, some say it's the spirit of the forest speaking, reminding visitors of the power and mystery that these trees have held for generations.

One plant that looks innocent but has an intriguing story is the *Foxglove*, with its tall stalks covered in bell-shaped flowers. In the Black Forest, foxglove is associated with fairies and is sometimes called "fairy gloves." According to old tales, fairies would wear the blossoms on their fingers as tiny gloves, and they would use the flowers to cast spells or deliver messages to each other. It was also believed that if you picked a foxglove flower without asking the fairies' permission, you might wake up the next day feeling dizzy or confused as a punishment for disturbing their homes. Foxglove is beautiful but also very toxic, so even though it looks magical, it's a plant that should be admired from a distance.

The *Yew Tree* is one of the oldest and most mystical trees in the forest. With its dark, needle-like leaves and berries that look like tiny red jewels, the yew tree is steeped in mystery and legend. Yews can live for thousands of years, and some in the Black Forest are so old that people believe they have witnessed the rise and fall of entire villages. These trees were often found near old churches and cemeteries because they were said to guard the spirits of the dead. In ancient times, it was believed that yew trees held the power of both life and death, as parts of the tree are highly toxic, while other parts were sometimes used in traditional medicine. People would sit beneath the branches of a yew tree to think and reflect, feeling that the tree's long history could inspire wisdom.

Even the humble *Wild Strawberries* that grow in the clearings of the Black Forest have stories behind them. According to legend, wild strawberries were a favorite treat of the forest fairies, and picking them without leaving a few behind for these magical creatures was said to bring bad luck. Children in the Black Forest have grown up hearing stories about how leaving a small basket of strawberries at the edge of the woods could earn you the fairies' favor. Some people even believed that if you whispered your wish into a strawberry and left it as a gift for the fairies, they might grant your wish.

Among the magical trees, the *Silver Fir* stands out as a symbol of the Black Forest itself. This tall, majestic tree with its deep green needles and silver underside has inspired awe for generations. It was believed that the Silver Fir had the power to connect the earth with the sky, acting as a ladder that spirits and magical beings could use to travel between the two worlds. In winter, when the forest is covered in snow, the Silver Firs seem to shimmer, creating a scene that feels almost otherworldly. Some tales say that on the longest night of the year, known as the winter solstice, the spirits of the forest gather beneath the Silver Firs to celebrate, bringing with them a sense of wonder that fills the whole forest.

Even plants that might seem ordinary, like *Ferns*, have their own stories. Ferns grow in the damp, shady parts of the forest, their fronds unfolding in delicate spirals. According to legend, ferns hold a secret: they are said to bloom with invisible flowers that only appear for a brief moment on Midsummer's Eve. If you were lucky enough to see one of these hidden blooms, it was said that you would gain the power to find lost treasures or see things that are usually hidden from human eyes, like fairy paths or hidden doors to magical realms. Young explorers in the Black Forest love to search for the secretive "fern flower," even though few have ever claimed to see it.

Bluebells, with their tiny, bell-shaped blue flowers, are often called "fairy thimbles" and are said to be used by fairies as hats or tiny cups for holding dew. The soft, delicate scent of bluebells filling the air is thought to signal that fairies are nearby. Children in the Black Forest know that you should never pick bluebells or step into a circle of them, as it might disturb the fairies and bring their mischievous tricks upon you. The sight of a patch of bluebells glowing in a shaft of sunlight is one of the most magical views in the forest, as if nature itself is reminding you that this is a place of wonders.

The Black Forest is truly alive with stories and magic, and its plants and trees are more than just parts of the landscape—they are characters in an endless tale of mystery and enchantment. For those who wander its paths, every leaf and branch has a story to tell, and every shadow might be the hiding place of a fairy, a sprite, or the spirit of an ancient tree.

Chapter 7: The Oldest Castles in the Forest

The Black Forest, with its deep woods and misty hills, has long been home to stories of knights, kings, and daring adventures. Hidden among the towering trees and rolling hills are the remains of some of Germany's oldest and most enchanting castles. These ancient stone structures have stood for hundreds of years, watching over the forest as the world changed around them. For young adventurers who love stories of kings, queens, and brave knights, visiting or learning about these castles is like stepping back into the pages of a storybook filled with mystery and excitement.

One of the most famous and oldest castles in the Black Forest is *Hohenzollern Castle*. Perched high on a hilltop that rises above the trees, this castle looks like it could be the home of a fairytale king. While the current version of Hohenzollern Castle was built in the 19th century, the original structure dates back to the 11th century, when it was a stronghold for the powerful Hohenzollern family. This family would later become one of the most influential dynasties in German history, ruling over parts of the country for many centuries. The castle has tall towers and stone walls that look out over the forest and surrounding villages. From its highest points, you can see for miles, with the forest stretching out like a sea of green waves. It's easy to imagine knights in shining armor standing guard and looking out for signs of approaching visitors or danger.

Another castle with a fascinating history is *Rötteln Castle*. Rötteln was built in the 11th century and, although it now lies in ruins, it once stood as a strong and mighty fortress that defended the region. The castle was constructed with thick stone walls, tall towers, and deep dungeons, making it an impressive sight that would have struck awe into anyone who approached it. As you explore what remains of

Rötteln Castle today, you can still climb up the old stone steps to the top of one of the towers and see the forest from above, just like medieval sentries did centuries ago. People say that if you listen closely, especially on a windy day, you might hear the whispers of ancient stories carried by the breeze, tales of knights and nobles who once walked these same paths.

Hochburg Castle is another gem of the Black Forest that dates back to the 11th century. Located near the town of Emmendingen, this castle was once one of the largest and most important fortresses in the region. It was originally built to protect the surrounding lands and served as a symbol of power for the local lords. The castle was strong enough to survive many battles and sieges, but over time, it fell into ruin as newer, stronger fortresses were built elsewhere. Today, visitors can walk among its towering stone walls, peek through the remains of arched windows, and wander into what used to be the grand halls and rooms where noble families lived. Exploring Hochburg Castle is like playing a game of hide-and-seek with history; you never know when you might stumble across an old carving or a stone stairway that leads to a hidden corner filled with mystery.

Deep within the forest is the old *Altensteig Castle*, a castle that looks as if it's been taken straight from a fairytale. Built in the 12th century, Altensteig Castle sits on a steep hill overlooking the small town of Altensteig. It has been very well preserved compared to many other ancient castles, which makes it feel even more magical. The castle's towers, made of stone and timber, have watched over the town and the forest for centuries. In the past, this castle would have been home to lords and ladies who ruled over the surrounding lands. The castle's rooms were filled with the sounds of medieval life: the clanging of armor, the soft melodies of minstrels playing their songs, and the laughter of people at grand feasts. Some stories say that on quiet nights, you can still hear the echoes of those sounds if you stand near the castle and close your eyes.

One of the more mysterious castles in the Black Forest is *Zavelstein Castle*. Built in the early 13th century, Zavelstein was once a grand fortress that was home to knights and noble families. Today, it stands mostly in ruins, with crumbling stone walls and towers that tell stories of the past. Zavelstein Castle is especially famous for its tower, which still stands tall and can be climbed for an incredible view of the Black Forest below. The tower gives you a sense of what life might have been like for the sentinels who watched the land from high above. Legends say that hidden within the castle's ruins are secret passages and rooms that were once used to hide treasure or provide an escape during times of danger. Some explorers and historians believe there might still be hidden chambers that have yet to be discovered, filled with old coins, armor, or other relics from long ago.

Burg Husen is another castle worth mentioning, with its history that stretches back to the 12th century. Located near the town of Hausach, Burg Husen was an important fortress during the Middle Ages. It was built to guard over important trade routes that passed through the Black Forest. The castle's location, high up on a rocky outcrop, made it a perfect spot for knights to watch for approaching travelers or potential invaders. While much of the original castle has been lost to time, parts of its walls and the watchtower remain standing. Climbing up to these remains, young adventurers can look out over the surrounding valleys and forests, imagining what it must have been like to live there when the castle was in its prime. People in the area tell stories of hidden treasures buried by the castle's former lords, who hid their wealth when they feared it would be stolen during attacks.

Windeck Castle is a castle that has stood in the Black Forest since the 12th century. Though now in ruins, it has a special charm that makes it feel alive with stories of the past. Windeck was once a powerful fortress that defended the region against invaders, with strong stone walls and high towers that were difficult to breach. Today, visitors can still see parts of these walls and climb the old, weathered steps to get a view of the surrounding forest. The castle ruins are covered in ivy and moss, which gives them a mysterious, enchanted feel. Children who visit Windeck Castle might find themselves imagining they're knights preparing to defend their home or princes and princesses watching for guests arriving from the edge of the woods.

The *Ruins of Hohenbaden*, also known as Old Castle, is another ancient structure that was built in the 12th century. Located near the town of Baden-Baden, Hohenbaden Castle was once a mighty fortress that overlooked the Rhine Valley. The castle's thick walls, tall watchtowers, and massive halls were home to the Margraves of Baden, who ruled over the land for many years. Although much of the castle has crumbled, visitors can still explore its rooms, winding staircases, and hidden corners. One of the most fascinating parts of Hohenbaden Castle is its "wind harp," a giant musical instrument that plays when the wind passes through it, creating haunting, beautiful melodies that fill the air. Hearing this music while exploring the castle adds to the feeling that the place is alive with stories and magic from long ago.

One castle that is wrapped in mystery is *Schwarzenburg Castle*. While not as well-known as some of the other castles in the Black Forest, Schwarzenburg has its own unique charm. Built in the 11th or 12th century, it was once an important fortress that guarded the surrounding area. Today, the castle stands in partial ruin, with its stone walls covered in green vines and wildflowers. Legends tell of hidden tunnels beneath the castle that once allowed its occupants to escape or move unnoticed during times of war. Some people believe that these tunnels still exist, buried beneath the earth, waiting to be discovered by an adventurous soul brave enough to go looking.

Finally, *Yburg Castle* is one of the Black Forest's oldest and most intriguing castles. Perched on a hill surrounded by vineyards and forest, Yburg was built in the 13th century and served as a stronghold for local nobles. The castle's stone walls and towers, which have seen countless seasons pass, are steeped in history. Yburg was known for being a place where feasts and celebrations were held, with nobles from nearby villages gathering for grand events. Today, parts of the castle remain intact, and visitors can wander through the stone hallways and peer out over the surrounding countryside. Stories say that Yburg Castle is home to friendly ghosts who roam the halls at night, revisiting their old rooms and whispering old tales to the wind.

These castles, with their high towers, secret passageways, and crumbling stone walls, are more than just ruins—they are pieces of history that tell stories of bravery, mystery, and magic. Each castle holds its own secrets, from hidden treasure to legendary ghost stories, and exploring them is like stepping into a time machine that takes you back to an era when knights defended their homes and nobles held feasts in great halls. The Black Forest is not only a place of natural beauty but also a land where the past comes alive, waiting for young explorers to uncover its stories and imagine the people who once called these castles home.

Chapter 8: Discovering Waterfalls and Lakes

The Black Forest is a magical place, not just because of its ancient trees and stories of knights and fairies, but also because of its sparkling waterfalls and shimmering lakes. These natural wonders are like hidden gems that add to the beauty and mystery of the forest. Discovering these waterfalls and lakes is an adventure that takes you through winding forest trails, over moss-covered rocks, and into clearings where the air is fresh and cool. For young explorers, visiting these special places is like finding secret spots where nature shows off its most magical sides.

One of the most famous waterfalls in the Black Forest is the *Triberg Waterfalls*. These falls are the tallest in Germany and are made up of seven cascading steps that tumble down a rocky hillside. The water rushes down with a powerful roar, splashing onto rocks and sending up a fine, misty spray that catches the sunlight and creates tiny rainbows. The sound of the water crashing down is both exciting and soothing, filling the forest with its constant, rhythmic noise. The path that leads to the top of the falls winds through the trees, with little bridges and platforms where you can stop and watch the water as it rushes by. The surrounding area is filled with tall pines and firs, and if you're lucky, you might spot a squirrel darting through the branches or hear the call of a bird. People say that at night, when the forest is quiet and the moonlight reflects off the water, the Triberg Waterfalls look almost magical, as if they belong in a fairy tale.

Not far from Triberg is another beautiful spot, *Todtnau Waterfall*. This waterfall is one of the oldest known in Germany and has been a popular place for visitors for many years. The water rushes down from a height of about 97 meters, creating a sparkling white curtain against the dark green of the forest. Todtnau Waterfall is surrounded by a variety of plants and flowers that grow in the damp soil, making the area feel lush and full of life. The cool air near the waterfall is a refreshing break from the warm summer sun, and it's easy to imagine that tiny forest fairies might live nearby, hiding under the ferns and mossy rocks. The path to the waterfall is an adventure on its own, with wooden bridges and steps that make it feel like you're on a quest to find a secret treasure.

Another waterfall that young adventurers would enjoy discovering is the *Allerheiligen Waterfalls*, also known as the All Saints Waterfalls. These falls are hidden in a gorge surrounded by the forest, and they're reached by following a narrow path that winds between the trees and over wooden bridges. The sound of the water splashing down the rocks gets louder as you get closer, and soon you'll see the water cascading down a series of steps, sparkling in the dappled sunlight that filters through the leaves. The Allerheiligen Waterfalls are especially beautiful in the spring when the water is at its fullest, and the surrounding plants are bright and green. Nearby, there are the ruins of an old monastery, which makes the area feel even more magical and mysterious. Imagine monks walking through the forest centuries ago, hearing the same sounds of rushing water that you hear today.

One of the most enchanting lakes in the Black Forest is *Lake Titisee*. This lake is surrounded by hills covered in thick, dark forest, making it look like a picture from a storybook. The water is clear and blue, reflecting the sky and the trees that stand like guards around its edges. On sunny days, the lake sparkles under the sun, and boats drift lazily across the surface, carrying people who want to enjoy the view or fish for their dinner. In the summer, visitors can swim in the lake's cool waters, or rent a paddleboat and explore the nooks and crannies of its shoreline. In the winter, when the lake sometimes freezes over, it becomes a place where kids and families come to skate and play on the ice. Legend has it that if you look into the water at just the right moment, you might catch a glimpse of water sprites that live beneath the surface, playing and splashing when no one is looking.

Another lake that's full of stories and beauty is *Lake Mummelsee*. This high-altitude lake is surrounded by tall fir trees that seem to touch the sky. Mummelsee is famous for its legends, especially the story of the King of the Mummelsee, who is said to live in a crystal palace at the bottom of the lake. According to the legend, he is a powerful water spirit who watches over the lake and the forest, and on moonlit nights, he comes to the surface to dance on the water with the other spirits. The lake's surface is smooth and dark, reflecting the surrounding trees like a giant mirror. Visitors often walk the trail that circles the lake, stopping to enjoy the view or listen to the rustle of the wind through the trees. On clear days, you can see the mountains in the distance, standing proudly against the sky.

Feldsee is another lake that feels like a hidden treasure. This small, glacial lake sits at the foot of the Feldberg, the highest mountain in the Black Forest. It is surrounded by steep hills covered in dense forest, making it feel like a secret spot that only the most adventurous explorers find. The water is cold and clear, with a greenish tint from the trees that lean over its edges. Feldsee is a peaceful place, perfect for sitting quietly and listening to the sounds of the forest: the calls of birds, the rustling of leaves, and the gentle lap of water against the shore. In the past, people believed that magical creatures called nymphs lived in lakes like Feldsee, dancing on the water when no one was there to see them.

For those who love waterfalls, the *Zweribach Waterfalls* are another hidden gem in the Black Forest. The journey to reach these falls is an adventure through winding paths, past towering trees and over trickling streams. The falls themselves are tucked away in a deep part of the forest, where the sunlight filters through the leaves and makes the water sparkle. The sound of the water splashing down the rocks is a welcoming sign that you've found them, and it feels like you've discovered a secret place. The water here isn't as tall or as loud as at Triberg or Todtnau, but it has a peaceful, magical quality that makes you want to stay and watch it dance down the rocks.

The *Bühlertal Waterfalls* are another exciting spot for young explorers. These waterfalls are smaller but surrounded by beautiful plants and flowers. The trail to reach them winds through the forest and across little wooden bridges, making you feel like you're on an adventure through an enchanted woodland. The water at Bühlertal tumbles over rocks and pools in small, clear basins, perfect for dipping your toes in on a warm day. Some old stories say that forest elves live near waterfalls like these, using the pools as mirrors to check their tiny, glittering wings.

In addition to waterfalls and lakes, the Black Forest is home to many small, hidden ponds and streams that make the landscape feel even more magical. These quiet spots are where frogs croak and dragonflies dart across the surface of the water. Sometimes, if you're very still and very lucky, you might even spot a deer coming down to the water to drink or see a family of ducks gliding across a hidden pond. Each of these places has its own stories and legends, passed down from generation to generation. Some say that if you sit by a pond at dusk, you might hear whispers of the forest's secrets being shared between the trees and the water.

The *Gertelbach Waterfalls* are another series of beautiful, smaller waterfalls located in the northern part of the Black Forest. These falls are tucked away in a gorge, surrounded by mossy rocks and ferns that make the area feel like it's part of an enchanted garden. The water here flows over a series of rocky steps, creating a soft, continuous sound that adds to the peacefulness of the place. The path to the Gertelbach Waterfalls is lined with wildflowers in the spring and summer, making it feel like a magical pathway that could lead to a hidden fairy village.

Whether it's the crashing roar of the Triberg Waterfalls or the still, reflective waters of Lake Mummelsee, each waterfall and lake in the

Black Forest has its own character and stories. They are places where nature's magic comes alive, and where young explorers can imagine what it would be like to live in a world full of mystery and adventure. From the sound of the water rushing over rocks to the sight of a clear lake surrounded by trees, these places remind visitors that the Black Forest is more than just a forest; it's a land of wonders waiting to be discovered.

Chapter 9: Stories of Forest Fairies and Spirits

The Black Forest has long been known for its thick woods, towering trees, and mysterious glades, but what really makes it special are the countless stories passed down through generations about forest fairies and spirits. These tales are filled with magic and wonder, making it easy to imagine that the forest is alive with beings that can only be seen when the conditions are just right. For hundreds of years, people living near the forest have told stories of fairy lights that dance in the dark, mysterious figures that guide travelers to safety, and trickster spirits who play pranks on those who wander too far into the woods. For young adventurers, these stories make exploring the forest feel like stepping into a magical world where anything is possible.

One of the most well-known tales from the Black Forest is that of the *Waldgeister*, or forest spirits. These beings are said to be the guardians of the trees, streams, and all the living creatures within the forest. They are known to appear as shadowy figures that flit between the trees, with glowing eyes that watch over those who enter their realm. The Waldgeister are usually benevolent, helping lost travelers find their way back to safety. In some stories, they even leave small gifts like berries or wildflowers for kind-hearted people who respect the forest and treat it with care. However, if someone comes into the forest with the intention of causing harm or taking more than they need, the Waldgeister are said to play tricks to lead them astray, making them feel lost and confused until they promise to respect the woods.

Another popular story is that of the *Nixen*, or water fairies. These enchanting creatures are said to live in the lakes, ponds, and streams that crisscross the Black Forest. The Nixen are often described as beautiful beings with long hair that shimmers like water in the sunlight. They sing hauntingly beautiful songs that can be heard when the wind carries their voices through the forest, especially near lakes like Mummelsee. According to legend, these songs have magical powers and can draw people closer to the water. While some say the Nixen are playful and harmless, others tell stories of them luring travelers to the water's edge, where they might slip and fall in if they're not careful. To protect themselves, travelers were once advised to carry small charms made of twigs or stones carved with special symbols.

Lake Mummelsee itself has its own legend that adds to its mystical reputation. It is said that deep under the lake's surface, there is a crystal palace where the *King of the Mummelsee* resides. This powerful water spirit is believed to rule over the Nixen and all the creatures that live in the lake. On quiet, moonlit nights, people say you might catch a glimpse of him rising from the water, wearing a crown made of pearls and surrounded by shimmering lights. The king is said to be wise and fair, rewarding those who respect the lake and punishing those who try to harm it or take its treasures. Stories tell of fishermen who were granted safe passage and good catches after leaving offerings by the water, like a piece of bread or a small trinket.

The Black Forest is also known for its stories of the *Moosweibchen*, or moss maidens. These gentle forest fairies are said to live in the deepest, darkest parts of the forest, where moss grows thick and the trees stand tall like ancient giants. The moss maidens are caretakers of the forest's plants and animals, nurturing the young saplings and watching over nests hidden in the trees. They are usually friendly to humans, especially children who show kindness to the forest. According to the tales, moss maidens sometimes appear to those who are lost or in need of help, guiding them back to the path or showing them where to find food and water. They are often described as wearing green dresses made of leaves and moss, blending seamlessly into the forest so that only the keenest eyes can spot them.

One of the more mischievous spirits of the Black Forest is the *Kobold*, a creature known for its tricks and pranks. The Kobolds are said to be small, elf-like beings that live in hidden caves, tree hollows, or even under large rocks. They enjoy playing tricks on travelers, such as moving their belongings or making strange noises to scare them. However, despite their playful nature, the Kobolds are not usually dangerous. In fact, there are stories of people who have gained the friendship of a Kobold by leaving them small gifts like shiny coins or bits of food. Once a Kobold is pleased, it might help its human friend by showing them hidden paths through the forest or protecting them from harm. Some tales even speak of Kobolds helping woodcutters by sharpening their axes overnight or leaving bundles of kindling ready for the fire.

One of the most mysterious beings said to inhabit the Black Forest is the *Schwarzwaldgeist*, or Black Forest spirit. This figure is said to be as old as the forest itself and is often depicted as a tall, shadowy figure with glowing eyes that seem to know everything that happens within the forest. The Schwarzwaldgeist is considered both a protector and a judge, watching over the forest and ensuring that balance is maintained. According to legend, if the forest is threatened, the Schwarzwaldgeist will appear to defend it, summoning wind, rain, and even wild animals to drive away those who wish to harm it. Despite its fearsome reputation, the Schwarzwaldgeist is also known to help those who show respect for the forest, rewarding them with good luck or safe travels.

The *Wild Hunt* is another famous tale associated with the Black Forest. In this story, a ghostly group of hunters led by a powerful and mysterious figure, sometimes called *Wotan* or *Odin*, races through the forest at night on black horses with glowing red eyes. The hunt is said to be accompanied by the sound of barking hounds, the blowing of hunting horns, and the rustle of leaves as the ghostly riders pass by. Some say that seeing the Wild Hunt is a sign of great danger or change, while others believe that it brings good fortune to those who witness it and live to tell the tale. To avoid being swept away by the Wild Hunt, people used to say you should hide under a tree or lie down flat on the ground until the sounds pass. The idea of the Wild Hunt has inspired many spooky stories and adventures that kids tell each other around campfires, imagining what it would be like to catch a glimpse of the ghostly hunters as they race through the night sky.

A gentler and more heartwarming story is that of the *Heidelbeermädchen*, or blueberry girls. These fairies are said to live in patches of wild blueberries and protect the berries from being picked by greedy hands. According to the tales, the Heidelbeermädchen are tiny, with dresses the color of ripe blueberries and hair that looks like little leaves. When someone picks berries with care, leaving some for the forest animals and future growth, the Heidelbeermädchen are pleased and might grant the picker a small blessing, like extra-sweet berries or a tiny glimmer of blue light as a sign of their gratitude. Children in the Black Forest love to pretend they are searching for signs of the Heidelbeermädchen while picking blueberries, hoping to see a tiny sparkle of magic among the leaves.

Stories of the *Waldschrate*, or wood trolls, are also popular in the Black Forest. These beings are said to be larger than the average forest spirit and covered in bark and moss, making them look like moving trees. The Waldschrate are known to be protectors of the oldest and most sacred parts of the forest, places where humans rarely go. They are usually peaceful but can become fierce if their home is threatened. Some legends say that if you wander too deep into the woods and disturb the trees, you might hear the deep, rumbling voice of a Waldschrat telling you to leave. However, they are also known for their kindness to those who respect the forest, guiding them to safety or helping them find lost items.

The Black Forest's stories of fairies and spirits are as diverse as the forest itself. From the playful Kobolds to the watchful Schwarzwaldgeist, each tale adds to the sense of wonder that fills the air when you walk among the trees. These stories have been told and retold for centuries, keeping the magic of the forest alive and sparking the imagination of every new generation that hears them. As the wind whispers through the branches and the streams gurgle over rocks, it's easy to believe that somewhere, hidden among the leaves and shadows, the fairies and spirits of the Black Forest are watching, waiting, and living their enchanted lives.

Chapter 10: Black Forest Cakes and Sweet Treats

When people think of the Black Forest, they might picture tall, mysterious trees and magical legends, but did you know that the region is also famous for its mouthwatering cakes and sweet treats? The Black Forest has a rich tradition of making desserts that are so delicious, they have become famous all around the world. These treats are not only tasty but also full of history and stories that make them even more special. Let's dive into the world of Black Forest cakes and sweet treats and discover why they are loved by everyone who visits or hears about this enchanting place.

The most famous of all the treats from the Black Forest is the *Schwarzwälder Kirschtorte*, or Black Forest cake. This cake is so legendary that it has become a symbol of the region itself. But what makes a Black Forest cake so special? The cake is made of layers of rich, moist chocolate sponge cake filled with whipped cream and cherries. The cherries are not just any ordinary cherries; they are often soaked in a special cherry brandy called *Kirschwasser*, which gives the cake its unique, slightly boozy flavor. This brandy is made from the cherries that grow in the Black Forest region, and it's an essential ingredient that sets the authentic Black Forest cake apart from any other chocolate and cherry dessert.

The top of the cake is decorated with even more whipped cream, whole cherries, and a generous sprinkling of chocolate shavings. When you cut into a slice, you see the beautiful layers of chocolate cake, white cream, and bright red cherries, making it as delightful to look at as it is to eat. Each bite is a perfect combination of rich chocolate, sweet and tart cherries, and light, airy cream. This cake has a history that stretches back to the early 20th century, and some stories say that it was inspired by the traditional costumes worn by women in the Black Forest, which often featured dark dresses with white blouses and cherry-red hats called *Bollenhüte*. These hats are decorated with large, bright red pom-poms that resemble the cherries on top of a Black Forest cake.

But the Black Forest's reputation for sweets doesn't stop with the famous cake. There are many other traditional treats that showcase the region's love for all things sweet and delicious. One of these is *Kirschstrudel*, a type of pastry that combines the classic flavors of cherries and Kirschwasser with layers of flaky, golden pastry dough. The dough is rolled out thin and filled with a mixture of cherries, sugar, and sometimes nuts or spices. When it's baked, the outside becomes crispy and light, while the inside is warm and gooey. Kirschstrudel is often served with a dusting of powdered sugar on top and sometimes a dollop of whipped cream or a scoop of vanilla ice cream on the side.

Another popular treat from the Black Forest is *Hefezopf*, which is a sweet, braided bread that's perfect for breakfast or as an afternoon snack. Hefezopf is made from a rich dough that includes eggs, butter, and a touch of sugar, which gives it a light sweetness and a soft, fluffy texture. The dough is braided into a long loaf and baked until it's golden brown. Sometimes, it's sprinkled with pearl sugar or topped with almonds for an extra bit of crunch and sweetness. Kids and adults alike love slicing into a warm loaf of Hefezopf and spreading it with butter or jam.

One of the most charming and fun treats in the Black Forest is the *Schneeballen*, which means "snowball" in German. These round pastries are made from strips of dough that are shaped into a ball, fried until crispy, and then dusted with powdered sugar so that they look like snowballs. Schneeballen have been enjoyed in the region for hundreds of years, and while the traditional version is simply dusted with sugar, modern versions are often dipped in chocolate, drizzled with caramel, or filled with sweet creams and fruit flavors. The crunchy outside and sweet filling make Schneeballen a delightful treat for anyone who loves trying unique desserts.

 The Black Forest is also known for its *Lebkuchen*, a type of spiced gingerbread that is especially popular during the winter months and around Christmas. Lebkuchen is made with honey, spices like cinnamon, cloves, and ginger, and sometimes nuts or dried fruit. It has a warm, cozy flavor that makes it perfect for cold winter days when people gather around a fire with mugs of hot cocoa or tea. In the Black Forest, Lebkuchen is often baked in special shapes like hearts, stars, or bells, and decorated with icing or chocolate. Some versions are soft and chewy, while others are more like cookies with a crunchy bite.

 Stollen is another festive treat that has its roots in the Black Forest and other parts of Germany. This dense, sweet bread is filled with dried fruit, candied citrus peel, and nuts, and it's often flavored with a hint of rum or almond paste. Stollen is dusted with a thick layer of powdered sugar, giving it the look of freshly fallen snow. Traditionally, Stollen is made around Christmas, and each loaf is shaped to represent the baby Jesus wrapped in a blanket, making it not only a delicious treat but also a symbol of the holiday season. People in the Black Forest enjoy Stollen with hot drinks and share it with friends and family as part of their holiday celebrations.

 For those who love cookies, the Black Forest is home to some delightful varieties. *Spritzgebäck* is a type of buttery, melt-in-your-mouth cookie that is piped into different shapes like stars, circles, or S-shapes before being baked. These cookies are simple but delicious, with a rich, buttery flavor that makes them hard to resist. Sometimes, they are dipped in chocolate or decorated with sprinkles for a festive touch. Another type of cookie that's popular in the region is *Zimtsterne*, or cinnamon stars. These cookies are made with ground almonds and cinnamon, giving them a chewy texture and warm, spicy flavor. They are often topped with a simple white icing that adds just the right amount of sweetness.

Black Forest honey cake is another sweet delight that comes from the traditions of beekeeping in the region. The Black Forest is known for its wildflowers and forests that provide nectar for bees, resulting in rich, flavorful honey. Honey cake is made using this local honey and is often spiced with cinnamon and cloves, giving it a deep, aromatic flavor. The cake is moist and slightly sticky, perfect for enjoying with a glass of milk or a cup of tea. Some versions of honey cake include nuts or dried fruits, adding texture and extra bursts of flavor.

Visiting the Black Forest wouldn't be complete without trying some of its delicious chocolates. The region is famous for its high-quality, handcrafted chocolates, which are often made using traditional methods passed down through families. Chocolatiers in the Black Forest create everything from creamy truffles filled with local cherry liqueur to chocolate bars studded with hazelnuts and dried berries. Some shops even make chocolates shaped like the forest animals or the famous cuckoo clocks, making them not only delicious but also fun to look at. The rich, smooth chocolate paired with unique flavors like marzipan, caramel, and fruit fillings makes Black Forest chocolate a special treat that is cherished by anyone who loves sweets.

When it comes to sweet drinks, the Black Forest doesn't disappoint. Hot chocolate made with rich, dark chocolate and topped with whipped cream is a favorite, especially during the colder months. For a traditional Black Forest twist, some recipes include a dash of Kirschwasser to give it a warming cherry flavor. Children and adults alike enjoy sipping on hot chocolate while taking in the beauty of the forest in winter, when snow covers the trees and makes everything look like a scene from a fairy tale.

The Black Forest's love for sweets is more than just about taste; it's also about tradition, family, and the stories that come with each recipe. Many of these desserts have been made in homes for generations, with recipes that are passed down from grandparents to parents to children. Baking together is a cherished activity, where families share stories, laughter, and the joy of creating something delicious. The smells of chocolate, cherries, cinnamon, and warm bread fill kitchens, making everyone feel cozy and connected.

Exploring the sweet treats of the Black Forest is like taking a journey into the heart of the region's culture. Each dessert has its own story, whether it's the history behind the Black Forest cake or the legends tied to the ingredients like cherries and honey. These treats are a reminder that the Black Forest is a place where nature, tradition, and magic come together to create not just beautiful landscapes and enchanting stories, but also flavors that are unforgettable.

Chapter 11: How the Forest Changes Through the Seasons

The Black Forest is a place full of wonder and mystery, and one of the most magical things about it is how it changes throughout the year. As the seasons pass, the forest transforms in ways that can make you feel like you're seeing a completely different place each time you visit. From the first buds of spring to the deep snow of winter, the forest goes through so many changes that it's almost like it has its own set of stories for each season. Let's go on a journey through the year and see how the Black Forest shifts and changes, bringing new sights, smells, and sounds with each season.

In the spring, the forest awakens after the long, cold winter. The snow begins to melt, feeding the streams and rivers that run through the forest, making them rush and sparkle as they carry the icy water away. The sound of trickling water fills the air, mixing with the songs of birds returning from their winter migration. This is the season of rebirth, and you can see it in the way green shoots push up from the ground, tiny wildflowers start to bloom, and the trees begin to sprout new leaves. The once-bare branches come alive with soft, pale green leaves that seem to grow bigger and brighter each day. The forest floor, which looked dark and lifeless in winter, becomes a carpet of green moss and colorful flowers. The sweet smell of blossoms fills the air, and bees buzz from flower to flower, starting their important work of pollination. Animals that have been in hibernation, like hedgehogs and dormice, begin to wake up and search for food, adding to the bustling energy of the season.

Spring is also the time when many of the forest's animals have their young. If you walk quietly, you might see a mother deer with her fawns hidden among the trees, their spots blending in perfectly with the dappled sunlight on the forest floor. Birds build nests high in the branches, and if you're lucky, you might catch a glimpse of tiny chicks peeking out, waiting for their parents to bring them food. The streams and ponds come alive with frogspawn that will soon become tadpoles and then frogs, adding their croaks to the chorus of sounds that echo through the trees. The forest feels like it's full of new life and promise, and every step you take feels fresh and exciting.

As spring turns to summer, the forest reaches its fullest and most vibrant state. The trees are thick with dark green leaves that create a canopy overhead, letting only dappled sunlight filter down to the forest floor. The days are warm and long, and the forest feels alive with activity. Animals are busy foraging for food, playing, and caring for their young. Squirrels dart up and down trees, chasing each other and nibbling on nuts, while foxes can sometimes be seen trotting through the underbrush. The streams are cool and inviting, perfect for a refreshing splash on a hot day. In the deeper parts of the forest, the air is cool and filled with the earthy smell of damp leaves and moss. Mushrooms begin to pop up in shaded spots, with some looking like tiny umbrellas and others taking on odd shapes and colors that seem almost magical.

Summer is also the time when the forest's plants and trees are in full bloom. Wildflowers of all colors grow in sunny clearings, attracting butterflies that flutter from one to another, adding splashes of bright color as they go. The sound of crickets and cicadas fills the warm afternoon air, creating a constant background song that makes the forest feel even more alive. Berries start to ripen in the summer sun, and if you know where to look, you can find wild strawberries and blueberries hidden among the leaves. These small, sweet treats are favorites not just for people but also for the animals of the forest, who come to snack on them when they are at their juiciest.

As the warm days of summer give way to the cooler temperatures of autumn, the forest begins to change again. This is one of the most breathtaking transformations of the year. The green leaves that have shaded the forest all summer long start to turn brilliant shades of yellow, orange, and red. The whole forest looks like it has been painted with a brush dipped in gold and crimson. As the leaves change color, they begin to fall, creating a rustling carpet that crunches underfoot. The crisp air carries the scent of fallen leaves and wood smoke from nearby cottages, where people are lighting their first fires of the season to keep warm. It's a time when the forest feels quieter, more peaceful, as if it's preparing for the long rest of winter.

Autumn is also harvest time, and the forest is full of ripe nuts, seeds, and fruits. Squirrels busily gather acorns and store them away for the winter, while wild boars root through the fallen leaves in search of chestnuts and other tasty treats. The deer, now fully grown, can often be seen grazing in open meadows, their coats thickening to prepare for the cold months ahead. Fungi become more prominent in autumn as well, and some of the most interesting mushrooms appear, with their bright colors and strange shapes. The forest during autumn is a feast for the senses, with the brilliant colors, the smell of earth and wood, and the sound of rustling leaves creating an unforgettable experience.

Then, winter arrives, and with it, the forest changes once more. The leaves have all fallen, leaving the trees bare and stark against the pale winter sky. The once-busy streams slow down, and some may even freeze over, creating patches of ice that glisten in the weak sunlight. Snow begins to fall, blanketing the forest in white and making everything look like a scene from a fairy tale. The forest becomes quiet and still, as many of the animals have gone into hibernation or have moved to lower, warmer areas. The only sounds might be the creaking of trees in the wind or the soft thump of snow falling from branches.

Despite the quiet, the Black Forest in winter is full of beauty and wonder. Animal tracks can be seen in the snow, telling the story of who has passed by—a deer looking for food, a fox on the hunt, or perhaps a hare dashing across an open space. Birds that stay for the winter, like woodpeckers and jays, add spots of color to the otherwise white and gray landscape. The forest looks almost otherworldly, with icicles hanging from branches like crystal ornaments and the snow creating a muffled, peaceful silence.

In winter, the people who live near the forest often tell stories and legends to pass the long, cold nights. The Black Forest has many tales about mysterious creatures and forest spirits that seem to come alive in the stillness of winter. The trees, stripped of their leaves, take on new shapes, casting long, eerie shadows on the snow. If you stand quietly and listen, you might even hear the creaking and groaning of the old trees, as if they're telling stories of their own about the many winters they have seen.

As winter slowly gives way to spring, the cycle starts over again. The first signs of new life appear with tiny green shoots poking up through the melting snow, and the sound of running water returns as the ice thaws. The forest shakes off its blanket of snow, waking up from its long sleep and starting the cycle all over again.

Each season in the Black Forest brings its own special kind of magic. From the new life of spring to the deep colors of autumn and the quiet, snowy peace of winter, the forest is always changing. This constant transformation makes it a place that feels alive, full of stories, and ever-ready to share its wonders with anyone who steps into its enchanting embrace. The forest teaches that change is natural and beautiful, and every season has its own story to tell.

Chapter 12: Meet the People Who Live in the Forest Villages

The Black Forest is not just a place of tall trees, ancient legends, and breathtaking landscapes; it is also home to many small villages where people have lived for centuries. These villages are like tiny pockets of life nestled among the trees, where the forest and the people share a special relationship. The people who live in the Black Forest villages are known for their strong sense of tradition, their connection to nature, and their welcoming spirit. They know the forest better than anyone and have learned how to live in harmony with it, taking only what they need and giving back in their own way. Let's step into these forest villages and meet the people who make them such special places.

One of the first things you'll notice about the people in the Black Forest villages is how deeply they respect their environment. They have a long history of living off the land, using the forest for its resources while making sure not to harm it. Many families have lived in the same village for generations, passing down not only their homes and traditions but also their knowledge of the forest and its secrets. They know which mushrooms are safe to eat and where to find wild herbs that can be used in cooking or to make natural remedies for colds and other ailments. Their connection to the forest is almost magical, and they teach their children from a young age how to respect and care for it.

The houses in these villages are something to marvel at. They are often made of wood and stone, with steep roofs that help the snow slide off in the winter. Some of the oldest houses have wooden beams that have darkened over time and are carved with intricate designs. Many homes have colorful shutters and window boxes overflowing with flowers like geraniums and petunias in the warmer months. These houses seem to blend seamlessly with the landscape, as if they grew right out of the forest itself. In the winter, snow covers the rooftops, and smoke curls up from chimneys, giving the villages a cozy, storybook look. Inside these homes, you'll find warm, wood-paneled rooms with old, hand-carved furniture, and big fireplaces that become the heart of the house during the cold months.

The people in the forest villages have many special skills and crafts that they have passed down through the years. One of the most famous crafts from this region is the making of cuckoo clocks. The art of crafting these clocks started hundreds of years ago, and it is still practiced by skilled artisans today. Each cuckoo clock is a masterpiece, carved with tiny details of animals, trees, and scenes from daily life in the Black Forest. Watching a craftsman at work is fascinating; they use tools to carve intricate patterns into wood and carefully assemble the tiny mechanisms that make the clock come to life. When the clock chimes and a little wooden cuckoo pops out to call the hour, it's like a small piece of the forest has been captured in a box.

Another important craft in the Black Forest is woodcarving. Villagers create everything from small wooden toys to large sculptures of animals and people. Some of the carvings tell stories of the old legends that have been passed down, like tales of forest spirits and brave hunters. During festivals, you might even see woodcarving competitions, where the best carvers show off their skills and create stunning pieces in just a few hours.

The people who live in the forest villages also have a deep love for music and dance. Traditional Black Forest music often includes instruments like accordions and violins, and the songs have a lively, cheerful beat. Many of the songs tell stories of life in the forest, from hunting deer to picking wild berries. During special events and festivals, the whole village comes together to sing and dance, dressed in traditional clothing. For the men, this might mean wearing leather trousers called *lederhosen*, and for the women, it means colorful dresses with aprons and hats decorated with large, fluffy pom-poms called

Bollenhüte. These hats are usually red if the woman is unmarried and black if she is married, making them not just beautiful but also meaningful.

Festivals in the Black Forest villages are times of joy and celebration. The biggest festivals are often tied to the seasons or religious holidays, like Christmas or harvest time. During these festivals, the streets are filled with laughter and music, and there are stalls selling handmade crafts, delicious food, and sweet treats like *Lebkuchen* (spiced gingerbread) and *Schneeballen* (pastry balls covered in sugar or chocolate). One of the most magical times of the year is Christmas, when the villages are lit up with twinkling lights and decorated with evergreen wreaths and wooden nativity scenes. In the evenings, families gather around their fireplaces, sipping on warm drinks like spiced cider or hot chocolate, and tell stories passed down through the generations.

Food is an important part of life in the forest villages, and the recipes have been perfected over generations. Traditional dishes are often made with ingredients that come from the forest itself, such as mushrooms, berries, and game. One famous dish is *Sauerbraten*, a pot roast that is marinated for days before being slow-cooked to create a rich, hearty flavor. Another favorite is *Schwarzwälder Schinken*, or Black Forest ham, which is smoked over pine wood and has a deliciously unique taste. The villagers are also known for their baking, making bread and pastries that fill the air with the warm, inviting smell of fresh dough. Bakeries in the villages often display rows of crusty loaves, soft pretzels, and of course, slices of Black Forest cake.

Life in the Black Forest villages isn't just about work and tradition, though. The people here know how to enjoy the simple pleasures of life. On weekends, families might go for long walks in the woods, gathering wildflowers and listening to the sounds of the forest. Children play by the streams, making tiny boats out of sticks and leaves and watching them float down the water. In the autumn, families go out to collect chestnuts and watch as the leaves turn golden and red. In winter, when the snow is thick and soft, children bundle up and go sledding down the gentle hills, their laughter ringing out through the crisp, cold air.

The older members of the villages are respected as keepers of history and tradition. They have stories about what life was like when they were young, tales of how their parents and grandparents survived harsh winters and celebrated good harvests. These stories are told around the fireplace or during village gatherings, where everyone sits together and listens. The elders also share important lessons, like which plants have medicinal properties and how to tell when a storm is coming by the way the birds behave. They are like living books, full of wisdom that helps the younger generations stay connected to their roots and to the forest that surrounds them.

The children of the Black Forest villages grow up with a special kind of freedom. They learn about the forest from a young age, playing in its shadow and exploring its hidden paths. They learn to climb trees, spot animal tracks, and recognize the songs of different birds. Parents teach them how to fish in the clear, cold streams and how to be safe while wandering through the woods. These children grow up with a deep love for the natural world, feeling a connection to the forest that stays with them for their entire lives.

As modern life brings changes to the world, the people of the Black Forest villages work hard to keep their traditions alive. While they have adapted to some of the conveniences of today, they are careful not to lose the old ways that make their villages so special. They still gather to celebrate festivals, teach their children how to carve wood and bake bread, and pass down stories that are as old as the trees around them. Visitors to the Black Forest often say that stepping into one of these villages feels like going back in time, where life is slower, simpler, and full of traditions that celebrate the beauty of the forest and the community.

The people of the Black Forest villages are guardians of a way of life that is both peaceful and full of stories. Their days are marked by the rhythms of nature, the changing seasons, and the traditions that they hold dear. Whether they are crafting cuckoo clocks, dancing in colorful costumes, or simply taking a walk through the trees, the villagers carry with them a deep respect for their home. They are a reminder that life close to nature can be rich, joyful, and filled with wonder, just like the forest that surrounds them.

Chapter 13: Secret Caves and Underground Wonders

The Black Forest is a place of mystery and wonder, known for its towering trees, rolling hills, and enchanting legends. But there is a whole other world hidden beneath the surface, where secret caves and underground wonders wait to be discovered. These hidden places are like nature's own treasure chests, filled with incredible rock formations, glistening crystals, and tunnels that seem to go on forever. Exploring these caves is like stepping into a different universe, one that feels both magical and a little bit spooky. Let's dive into the stories and secrets of the caves and underground marvels of the Black Forest.

Imagine walking through a dense part of the forest, where the trees are so close together that only specks of sunlight manage to reach the ground. Suddenly, you notice a small opening tucked between rocks, partially hidden by ferns and moss. This entrance could lead to one of the many caves in the Black Forest, each with its own unique story. Some caves are well known and have been visited by people for hundreds of years, while others remain untouched, only explored by the curious animals that call the forest home.

One of the most famous caves in the Black Forest is the *Erdmannshöhle*, also known as the Earth Man's Cave. This cave is one of the oldest in Germany, and its formation began millions of years ago. When you step inside, the air feels cool and damp, and the sound of dripping water echoes through the dark. The cave walls are lined with stalactites, which hang from the ceiling like icicles, and stalagmites, which rise up from the floor like ancient stone pillars. Some of these formations are so large that they look like the columns of a grand, underground cathedral. The shapes seem almost alive, as if the cave is frozen in the middle of a dance that has taken millions of years to unfold. In the dim light, your imagination can run wild—are those stone figures really just rocks, or could they be the spirits of the forest turned to stone?

Not far from the Earth Man's Cave is another fascinating underground wonder called the *Teufelsloch*, or Devil's Hole. Legend has it that this cave got its name because people believed it was a gateway to the underworld. The cave is deep and narrow, with twisting tunnels that can feel endless. If you venture inside, you'll notice that the sound changes—the deeper you go, the more muffled everything becomes, as if the cave is swallowing up the noise. Some villagers say they've heard strange whispers coming from the depths of the cave on quiet nights, but most believe it's just the wind moving through the narrow passages. Still, the stories add an air of mystery that makes this cave even more intriguing.

The Black Forest is also home to caves that sparkle and shine with the beauty of crystals. The *Falkensteiner Höhle* is one such place, where explorers can find walls that glitter with quartz and other minerals. The crystals catch the light and reflect it in a dazzling display, making it look like the cave is covered in stars. This cave is a favorite among those who love to imagine treasure hidden deep in the earth. Long ago, people believed that gnomes and other mythical creatures lived in caves like these, guarding their hoards of gold and precious stones. While no one has ever proven that such creatures exist, the caves themselves are treasures, full of wonders that make you feel like you've stepped into a fairy tale.

One of the most mysterious underground places in the Black Forest is a cave system known as *Höllenschlund*, or Hell's Maw. The entrance to this cave is wide and dark, and stepping inside feels like being swallowed by the earth. The cave is known for its narrow, twisting tunnels and deep chambers where no light reaches. Some parts of the cave are flooded, creating underground lakes and streams that reflect the light of a lantern like a mirror. The water in these hidden lakes is often so still that it looks like a sheet of glass, and it's said that if you stand quietly, you might see shadows moving across the surface, though no one knows what they are. The cave's name and eerie appearance have inspired many ghost stories, and it's easy to see why. The combination of silence, darkness, and mysterious reflections makes it feel like the cave holds secrets that are best left undiscovered.

Caves in the Black Forest are not just empty spaces; they are full of natural wonders that have taken thousands, sometimes millions, of years to form. The stalactites and stalagmites grow so slowly that it can take a century for one to grow just an inch. This makes you realize just how old the caves are and how much history they hold. Some caves have unusual rock formations that look like animals, faces, or even whole scenes, like a village carved in stone. Explorers often name these formations, and over time, the names become part of the cave's story. One famous formation in the Black Forest is called the *Dragon's Tongue*, a jagged piece of rock that looks like a dragon sticking out its tongue at visitors who dare to come close.

The caves are also home to some creatures that have adapted to life in the dark. Bats are the most common inhabitants, and they can often be seen hanging upside down from the ceiling, sleeping during the day and coming out at night to hunt for insects. These bats are harmless to people and play an important role in keeping the insect population under control. There are also tiny, pale insects and spiders that have evolved to live in complete darkness. These creatures are almost ghostly, with no need for eyes because there is no light underground. Seeing them makes you feel like you've discovered a secret world where life has learned to exist in the most unlikely places.

In some caves, explorers have found ancient drawings and carvings made by people who lived thousands of years ago. These early humans might have used the caves as shelters or for special ceremonies. The drawings often depict animals like deer and boars, as well as mysterious symbols that no one fully understands. Archaeologists study these markings to learn more about the people who once roamed the Black

Forest and how they connected with their environment. Finding these ancient artworks is like receiving a message from the past, a reminder that the forest and its caves have been a part of human life for as long as anyone can remember.

The people who live in the Black Forest villages have many stories and legends about the caves. They talk about hidden treasure guarded by ancient spirits and brave explorers who got lost in the dark tunnels, never to be seen again. Some caves are said to be homes to mythical creatures like dwarfs, who are expert miners and craftsmen. According to legend, these dwarfs are kind but very secretive, and they only show themselves to people who are pure of heart. If you happen to meet one, the stories say that they might share a bit of their treasure with you or teach you some of their ancient knowledge.

For many years, the caves of the Black Forest have also attracted adventurers and scientists who want to study their unique formations and ecosystems. These explorers often bring special equipment like ropes, helmets, and lights to help them navigate the dark, slippery passages. They map the caves, measure the rock formations, and even take samples to learn more about how the caves were formed. Sometimes, they find new chambers that no one has ever entered before, adding to the map of the underground world. These discoveries show that even though the surface of the Black Forest is well-known, its underground is still full of mysteries waiting to be uncovered.

Exploring a cave can be thrilling, but it also requires caution. The underground world is fragile, and touching the formations or making too much noise can disturb the delicate balance of the cave's ecosystem. Visitors are always reminded to tread carefully and respect the caves, taking only memories and leaving only footprints. The local guides who take people on tours know these caves inside and out, and they love to share their knowledge. They'll tell stories about the time they found an old tool buried in the dirt, or how they once spotted an albino salamander, a creature so rare that some people believe it brings good luck.

The caves of the Black Forest are places where time seems to stand still. They hold the history of the earth, carved into stone over millions of years, and the stories of people and creatures that have called them home. From sparkling crystal walls to deep, echoing chambers and hidden lakes, these underground wonders offer a glimpse into a world that is as mysterious as it is beautiful. They remind us that the Black Forest is not just what we see on the surface; it is a place of layers, each one hiding its own secrets, waiting to be discovered by those brave enough to step into the dark and explore.

Chapter 14: Ancient Myths and Famous Folktales

The Black Forest is full of stories that have been passed down for centuries, making it one of the most enchanting and mysterious places in Europe. These tales are told in whispers around campfires, shared by parents and grandparents on dark winter nights, and even written in old books with pages that crackle as you turn them. The myths and folktales of the Black Forest are filled with strange creatures, brave heroes, and magical events that spark the imagination. Let's take a journey into the heart of these stories and discover why they have fascinated people for so long.

One of the most famous myths is about *The Witch of the Black Forest*, a story that has both scared and amazed listeners for generations. The witch is said to live in a tiny, crooked house deep in the woods, hidden away where sunlight barely reaches. According to legend, she is as old as the forest itself, with hair as white as the snow and eyes that glow like embers. She knows all the secrets of the woods and can cast powerful spells. Some versions of the tale say she helps lost travelers find their way home, while others claim she tricks them into staying forever, turning them into animals or trees that blend into the forest. When children in the village hear about the witch, they shiver with a mix of fear and excitement. They know not to wander too far into the woods alone, just in case they find themselves at the witch's doorstep.

Another beloved tale is *The Spirit of the Silver Lake*, a story that takes place in a hidden lake said to be so clear that you can see straight to the bottom. In the tale, the lake is guarded by a spirit named Elara, who is as beautiful as the moon's reflection on the water. She wears a dress made of silver mist and moves as silently as the wind. People say that on moonlit nights, Elara rises from the lake to sing, her voice so haunting and lovely that it stops anyone who hears it in their tracks.

But there's a warning that comes with the story: if someone tries to capture her or take the treasures rumored to be hidden at the bottom of the lake, Elara will disappear in a whirl of mist, and the person will never find their way out of the forest again. This tale is told to remind children and adults alike that greed can lead to trouble and that some mysteries are best left alone.

The Black Forest is also famous for the legend of *The Giant King and His Golden Crown*. According to this tale, a giant named Wotan ruled the forest long before humans came to live there. He was so big that his footsteps left craters that later turned into small lakes and ponds. Wotan had a crown made of pure gold, which he wore day and night. It was said that this crown was enchanted and held the power of the forest—every tree, animal, and stream obeyed Wotan's command when he wore it. One day, a mischievous elf wanted to play a trick on the giant and stole the crown while he was sleeping. When Wotan awoke and found his crown missing, he roared so loudly that the mountains shook, and trees fell. He searched for the crown, but the elf was clever and hid it in a cave guarded by spells only he could break. The giant's search for the crown is said to have left the Black Forest full of hidden caves, twisting paths, and deep hollows where he stomped in anger. To this day, explorers who find mysterious caves believe they are searching the same places Wotan once did.

Another popular story is *The Tale of the Forest Fairies*, who are said to live in the deepest parts of the woods, where moss carpets the ground and sunlight dances through the leaves. These fairies are tiny, with wings like dragonflies that shimmer in shades of blue, green, and silver. They are playful but shy, and only those with the kindest hearts can see them. The story goes that long ago, a young woodcutter named Jakob stumbled upon a clearing filled with glowing lights while searching for firewood. He realized that the lights were actually fairies celebrating a festival under the moon. Jakob was so amazed that he dropped his axe and watched in awe. The fairies noticed him but, seeing that he was kind, invited him to join their dance. When the night ended, they gave Jakob a blessing: as long as he respected the forest and never harmed more trees than he needed, he would be able to find his way home no matter how deep he wandered into the woods. Jakob kept his promise, and the story became a lesson passed down to remind people to live in harmony with nature.

The Hunter and the White Stag is another tale that has been told for hundreds of years. It's about a skilled hunter named Lukas who boasted that he could catch anything in the forest. One day, a wise old man warned Lukas about the White Stag, a legendary creature with antlers that glowed like frost and eyes as bright as stars. It was said that the stag was the spirit of the forest, and anyone who tried to hunt it would be cursed. Lukas, proud and stubborn, didn't listen. He set out to find the stag, convinced he would be the one to catch it. After days of tracking, he finally saw it standing majestically in a sunlit clearing. Just as he raised his bow, the stag turned and looked at him. Its eyes seemed to speak, asking Lukas if he really wanted to harm something so beautiful. Lukas felt his heart change, and he dropped his bow. The stag nodded, as if understanding, and disappeared into the trees. Lukas returned to his village a wiser man, sharing the lesson that the forest was full of wonders that should be admired, not conquered.

There is also the tale of *The Enchanted Tree of Eternal Summer*. According to legend, there was once a tree in the Black Forest that never lost its leaves, even in the coldest winter. Its branches were covered with flowers and fruit all year round, and the air around it was warm and fragrant. People believed that whoever found the tree would have happiness and good fortune forever. Many searched for it, guided by stories passed down through generations. The story goes that the tree was guarded by a forest spirit named Liora, who only appeared to those who were pure of heart and kind to others. The few who claimed to have seen the tree said that it glowed softly, with petals that whispered like tiny bells when the wind blew. The story of the enchanted tree is often told to children, reminding them to be kind and generous, as it's believed that those with such hearts might one day find the tree and experience its magic.

Folktales also include stories of mysterious creatures like the *Black Forest Goblins*, who are mischievous but not always harmful. These goblins are said to live under old tree roots and in shadowy caves. They love playing tricks, like tying knots in horses' manes or making footprints that lead in circles to confuse travelers. However, the goblins are also known to help those who are lost, guiding them out of the forest if they feel they deserve it. There's one story about a girl named Greta who got lost picking berries. As night fell and she began to cry, tiny lights appeared around her. It was the goblins, who felt sorry for her and showed her the way back to her village, laughing and skipping along the path as they went. When Greta told her story, the villagers smiled and said that the goblins only help those who have a pure heart and good intentions.

One of the spookier legends is *The Phantom Rider*, a ghostly figure who is said to ride through the forest on stormy nights. He is described as wearing a dark cloak, with eyes that glow like coals and a horse that gallops so fast it seems to fly. Some stories say he is searching for something he lost long ago, while others claim he is the spirit of an old knight who was cursed to wander the forest forever. People say that if you see the Phantom Rider, you should not try to follow him, for doing so will lead you deeper into the forest until you are hopelessly lost. This story is told as a warning to those who think they are brave enough to venture into the woods on stormy nights.

The folktales and myths of the Black Forest are rich with lessons and morals. They teach about the importance of respecting nature, being kind, and listening to the wisdom of elders. They remind people that there is magic all around them if they take the time to see it. Even today, when people walk through the Black Forest and hear the rustling of leaves, the distant hoot of an owl, or the babbling of a hidden brook, they remember the stories and wonder if there might still be some truth in them. The forest, with its ancient trees and shadowy paths, holds its secrets close, inviting anyone who dares to listen to step into a world where myths come alive and folktales are not just stories, but a part of the landscape itself.

Chapter 15: Animals That Only Come Out at Night

As the sun sets over the Black Forest and the last rays of light disappear behind the mountains, the woods transform. The once bright and lively forest becomes a shadowy realm, full of mysterious sounds and movements. This is when the nocturnal animals, the creatures of the night, come out of hiding and take over the forest. Unlike the animals that are active during the day, these night-dwellers have special abilities and features that help them thrive in the dark. Let's take a closer look at the fascinating world of animals that only come out at night and how they make the Black Forest come alive under the stars.

One of the most famous nocturnal animals in the Black Forest is the owl. Owls are known for their eerie calls that echo through the night, sending shivers down the spines of those who hear them. The most common type in the Black Forest is the *tawny owl*, which has brown feathers that help it blend perfectly into the tree bark during the day. But it's at night that the owl's true powers shine. With eyes that are specially adapted to see in low light, owls can spot even the tiniest movement from high up in the trees. Their eyes are so powerful that they can see up to ten times better in the dark than humans can. But that's not all—owls also have incredible hearing. Their ears are positioned at slightly different heights on their heads, which allows them to pinpoint exactly where a sound is coming from. This makes them expert hunters, able to catch small animals like mice and voles with deadly precision.

The Black Forest is also home to a small, secretive animal called the *dormouse*. This little creature spends most of its day sleeping in a cozy nest made of leaves, hidden in the hollows of trees or dense bushes. But when night falls, the dormouse becomes active, scurrying through the underbrush in search of food. Dormice have big, round eyes that help them see in the dark, and their long, bushy tails help them balance as they climb. They are most active in the summer and fall when they collect seeds, nuts, and berries to store for the long winter hibernation. In stories and legends, dormice are often seen as symbols of quietness and secrecy, fitting perfectly into the mysterious nighttime world of the forest.

Bats are another well-known creature of the night, and the Black Forest is home to several different types. While some people might think bats are scary, they are actually quite amazing and play an important role in the forest ecosystem. Bats are the only mammals that can truly fly, and they come out at night to hunt for insects, including mosquitoes and beetles. One of the most common species in the Black Forest is the *common pipistrelle bat*, which is tiny—small enough to fit in the palm of your hand. These bats use a special skill called echolocation to find their food in the dark. They make high-pitched sounds that bounce off objects and return as echoes, telling the bat exactly where things are, like a natural sonar. This ability allows them to navigate the night sky and find their meals, even in complete darkness. Watching a bat flit through the air, zigzagging and swooping as it chases insects, is like seeing a tiny, silent acrobat perform under the moonlight.

Another nighttime wanderer is the *red fox*, a clever and adaptable animal that is active during both dusk and dawn, but most commonly at night. With its fiery red fur and bushy tail, the red fox moves quietly through the forest, searching for food. Foxes have excellent night vision and an acute sense of smell that helps them find their prey, which can include rabbits, birds, and even insects. Their large ears allow them to hear tiny rustlings in the grass from far away. Sometimes, if you are lucky and very quiet, you might spot a fox darting between the trees, its eyes glowing like small lanterns when they catch the moonlight. Foxes are also known for their playful nature and have even been seen playing games with each other under the stars.

One of the more mysterious night creatures of the Black Forest is the *pine marten*. These animals are part of the weasel family and are known for their sleek, slender bodies and sharp claws. Pine martens are excellent climbers and often spend their nights scampering through the trees, hunting for birds, eggs, and small mammals. They have thick, glossy fur that ranges from dark brown to almost black, with a pale yellow patch on their throat. Pine martens are shy and elusive, so spotting one is a rare treat. They are most active at night, when the forest is quiet and fewer predators are around. In some stories, pine martens are considered tricksters, known for their cleverness and ability to slip away into the shadows without a sound.

Then there are the *hedgehogs*, small, spiky creatures that shuffle through the forest at night, searching for food. Hedgehogs have poor eyesight, but their sense of smell and hearing make up for it, helping them find insects, worms, and fruit to eat. When they feel threatened, hedgehogs roll up into a tight ball, with their sharp spines sticking out in every direction to protect themselves from predators. If you're ever in the Black Forest on a quiet evening, you might hear the rustling of leaves and catch a glimpse of a hedgehog snuffling around, its tiny nose twitching as it hunts for its next meal. These little animals are a favorite among children and are often featured in fairy tales as friendly, helpful characters.

The *noctule bat* is another type of bat found in the Black Forest, but it's much larger than the common pipistrelle. Noctule bats are strong fliers and can often be seen at dusk, soaring high above the trees in search of moths and beetles. They are fascinating because of their social behavior; they often live in groups called colonies, which can be found in tree hollows or old buildings. Hearing the chirps and squeaks of bats as they communicate with each other adds an eerie soundtrack to a nighttime walk through the forest.

Among the less-seen creatures of the night are the *lynx*, a large, wild cat with tufted ears and a short tail. Though they are rarely spotted, their presence in the Black Forest adds to its mystery. Lynx are skilled night hunters, using their sharp eyesight and quiet movements to catch deer, rabbits, and birds. They are known for their patience, often waiting silently for the perfect moment to pounce on their prey. The lynx's fur is usually a mix of brown and black spots, which helps it blend into the forest floor and stay hidden. People who have seen the lynx say that it moves with a graceful, ghost-like quality, making it seem almost like a spirit of the forest itself.

The forest is also home to *fireflies*, tiny insects that light up the darkness with their bioluminescence. On warm summer nights, you can see them flickering through the trees like tiny, floating lanterns. The glow of a firefly is used to attract mates, but to those who watch them, it looks like a magical dance of lights moving through the underbrush. Fireflies are a favorite sight for anyone spending an evening in the Black Forest, adding a touch of wonder to the nighttime landscape.

Then there are the *badgers*, sturdy, striped creatures that live in underground burrows called setts. Badgers are mostly nocturnal, coming out at night to dig for worms, insects, and roots. They are known for their digging skills and strong, clawed paws that can move a surprising amount of earth. Badgers are social animals and often live in family groups, making the nighttime hours full of quiet rustles and snorts as they go about their nightly routines. Badger tracks are another clue that explorers can look for during a hike, and finding them is like uncovering a secret about the night life of the forest.

As you can see, the Black Forest is not silent at night; it's full of life and movement. From the hoots of owls and the rustling of dormice to the flickering lights of fireflies and the quiet scurrying of hedgehogs, the forest becomes a different world when the sun goes down. It's a place where the stars twinkle above, the trees cast long, twisting shadows, and every rustle or call seems to carry a story. The creatures that call the Black Forest home are perfectly adapted to the dark, each with unique abilities that help them survive and thrive when most of the world is asleep. Whether you're listening for the call of an owl or watching a bat swoop through the air, exploring the forest at night reveals a world that is just as full of wonder and mystery as it is during the day.

Chapter 16: Forest Music and Traditional Songs

In the heart of the Black Forest, where the towering trees sway gently and the air carries the scent of pine, there's something almost magical about the sounds that echo through the woods. But beyond the calls of birds and rustling leaves, there is another type of sound that brings the forest to life: music. For hundreds of years, the people living in and around the Black Forest have created songs and music inspired by their surroundings. These songs are not just notes and words; they are stories passed down through generations, capturing the spirit of the forest and the traditions of those who call it home.

Imagine standing in a small village nestled on the edge of the Black Forest as the sun begins to set. The windows of the cottages glow with the warm light of lanterns, and in the village square, musicians start to gather. The instruments they play have been part of the forest's history for as long as anyone can remember: wooden flutes carved by hand, fiddles with strings that sing out high, happy notes, and accordions that fill the air with a rich, full sound. As the first notes of a song drift into the air, people begin to tap their feet, and soon the whole village is caught up in the music.

One of the most well-known types of music in the Black Forest is folk music. This music tells stories of the land, the seasons, and the old tales that have been shared over countless firesides. These songs often have lively, upbeat melodies that make you want to dance, even if you're just listening. One popular traditional song is about the changing seasons in the forest. In spring, the song talks about new flowers pushing up through the earth and birds returning to build their nests. By summer, the music becomes faster, celebrating the warm, sunny days when children play in the meadows and farmers work in the fields. When autumn arrives, the music changes its tune to reflect the golden leaves that fall from the trees and the harvest celebrations that bring the village together. Finally, in winter, the songs slow down, becoming softer and more peaceful, as people gather indoors to keep warm and tell stories by the fire.

    These songs are often accompanied by dances, and many of them are easy to learn. Children in the villages grow up learning to clap their hands, stomp their feet, and move in circles as the music plays. The dances are just as much a part of the tradition as the songs themselves. One of the most fun dances is a circle dance called the *Reigen*, where everyone holds hands and moves in time with the music, spinning and laughing as they go. The older villagers like to teach the young ones, passing down not just the steps but the joy that comes with them. The dances often mimic the things seen in the forest: the flowing of a river, the scampering of a squirrel, or the flitting of birds from branch to branch.

    Beyond the village music, there is a special kind of sound that the forest itself seems to make. When the wind blows through the tall pines, it creates a gentle whistling noise, almost like a flute. Birds like the nightingale add their voices to the melody, their songs clear and sweet even in the dim light. And if you listen closely at night, you might hear the distant hoot of an owl or the call of a fox, each one adding a unique note to the natural symphony. In the old days, people believed that the forest was alive with spirits, and that these spirits made their own music to celebrate the beauty of nature. Stories were told of fairies playing tiny harps made of spider webs and elves drumming on hollow logs, adding to the mystery of the forest.

    Traditional songs of the Black Forest are also filled with stories of legendary characters. There are songs about brave hunters who ventured deep into the woods and found hidden treasures, and others about kind witches who helped lost children find their way home. One famous ballad tells the tale of a woodcutter named Hans who heard a haunting melody coming from deep within the forest. He followed the sound until he found a clearing where magical creatures were playing music that seemed to make the trees themselves dance. When he returned to the village and tried to describe what he had seen, the words escaped him, so he made a song instead. That song was passed down through generations and is still sung today, reminding everyone that there are wonders in the forest that can only be discovered by those who listen carefully.

The instruments used in traditional Black Forest music are often made from the very materials found in the forest. The wooden flute, for instance, is carved from the branches of elder trees, which are said to have magical properties in folklore. The sound of the flute is soft and airy, perfect for playing melodies that mimic birdsong or the whispering of the trees. The accordion, with its bellows and buttons, was introduced later but became a favorite because of its ability to play both joyful and melancholic tunes. The zither, a stringed instrument that rests on the musician's lap, produces delicate, twinkling notes that remind listeners of a bubbling stream or the twinkling stars above.

Festivals are an important time for music in the Black Forest, and each one has its own special songs. During the harvest festival, musicians play cheerful tunes to celebrate the gathering of crops and the end of hard work in the fields. Everyone comes together to sing and dance, sharing food and laughter late into the night. At Christmas, the music takes on a more sacred tone. Carols are sung in the village church, with voices rising up to the rafters, filling the space with warmth even as snow falls outside. These carols often speak of peace, hope, and the quiet beauty of the forest covered in white.

One unique tradition in the Black Forest is the *yodeling* that can be heard echoing through the hills. Yodeling is a way of singing that switches quickly between high and low notes, creating a sound that carries across long distances. It was originally used by shepherds to communicate from one mountainside to another, but over time, it became part of the music performed at gatherings and festivals.

Yodeling is playful and challenging, and it takes skill to do it well. When a group of yodelers sings together, their voices blend in a way that is both exciting and harmonious, filling the air with a sound that is uniquely their own.

Children in the villages love learning these songs and adding their own playful touches. It's common to see groups of friends pretending to be the characters in the songs—hunters, witches, and elves—while they sing and act out the stories. This helps keep the old tales alive and makes sure that even the youngest villagers know the songs by heart. Parents often sing lullabies to their children, songs that have been sung for generations. These lullabies are simple, with soft, soothing melodies that mimic the sound of the wind and the forest at night. They are filled with words that talk about dreams, stars, and the gentle rustling of leaves.

Sometimes, musicians come from outside the Black Forest to join in the celebrations, bringing new instruments and songs with them. But no matter how many new melodies are introduced, the traditional songs of the forest remain the most cherished. They are a reminder of the deep connection the people have with the land around them, a connection that goes back hundreds of years. These songs are a way of saying that the forest is not just a place but a part of who they are.

Even today, if you walk through the Black Forest on a warm summer night, you might catch the sound of a flute playing in the distance or the hum of a tune being carried by the breeze. It's as if the forest itself remembers all the songs and stories and whispers them to anyone who will listen. Music in the Black Forest is more than just entertainment; it's a celebration of nature, history, and the people who live among the trees. Whether through the happy notes of a fiddle, the haunting call of an owl, or the soft yodels echoing across the hills, the forest comes alive with the sounds of music, connecting everyone who hears it to a world full of wonder and tradition.

Chapter 17: Exploring the Black Forest by Bike

Exploring the Black Forest by bike is an adventure that mixes fun, exercise, and the thrill of discovering a place rich with history and natural wonders. For anyone who loves riding through winding paths, up gentle hills, and past beautiful scenery, the Black Forest is like a playground waiting to be explored. This forest, known for its dark, dense woods and fairy-tale charm, has miles and miles of trails that take riders through some of the most stunning landscapes in all of Germany. Biking through the Black Forest is more than just a ride; it's a journey through a land of legends, wildlife, and breathtaking views that change with every twist and turn of the path.

When you set out to bike through the Black Forest, the first thing you'll notice is how different each part of the forest can be. There are trails for everyone, from easy paths perfect for families with young children to challenging routes that climb steep hills and wind through thick woods. If you're a beginner, there are gentle, paved paths that take you along rivers and through sunny meadows filled with wildflowers. These paths are smooth and wide, making it easy to pedal along and enjoy the scenery without worrying about bumps or obstacles. One popular beginner trail is the *Kinzig Valley route*, which winds through small, picturesque villages and follows the path of the Kinzig River. As you ride, you might see ducks swimming in the river or spot a deer grazing in the distance.

For those who are a bit more experienced, the Black Forest offers more challenging paths that take you deeper into the heart of the forest. These trails often lead through dense clusters of tall pines and oaks, where the sunlight barely reaches the forest floor, creating a cool, mysterious atmosphere. As you pedal along, the air is filled with the fresh scent of pine needles, and the only sounds are the rustling of leaves and the occasional chirp of a bird or the chatter of a squirrel scurrying up a tree. The more challenging trails might have rocky patches or steep inclines that make your legs work hard, but reaching the top of a hill and seeing the view spread out below makes every push worth it. One such route is the climb up to *Feldberg*, the highest peak in the Black Forest. The ride to the top is steep and demanding, but once there, you're rewarded with a view that stretches all the way to the Alps on clear days.

One of the most exciting things about biking through the Black Forest is how much there is to discover along the way. Hidden in the woods are old castles and ruins that seem to appear out of nowhere, standing as reminders of stories from long ago. You might come across the ruins of *Hohengeroldseck Castle*, an ancient fortress that whispers tales of knights and battles. Stopping your bike to explore these old stone walls can feel like stepping back in time. Imagine walking through what was once the main hall, where knights feasted after returning from their adventures, or standing in a tower and imagining what it would have been like to look out over the forest centuries ago.

But the surprises don't stop with old castles. The Black Forest is also home to charming villages that seem almost frozen in time. As you pedal into one of these villages, you'll notice the wooden houses with their sloping roofs and colorful flower boxes spilling over with bright geraniums. These villages often have small bakeries where you can stop and try a slice of Black Forest cake, a treat layered with cherries, cream, and rich chocolate. Taking a break in a village like *Triberg* not only gives you a chance to rest your legs but also lets you experience the warm hospitality of the locals, who might share stories about the forest or tell you about their own favorite trails.

Another wonderful aspect of biking in the Black Forest is the variety of landscapes you'll see. One moment, you might be pedaling through an open meadow with butterflies flitting from flower to flower, and the next, you're entering a forest so dense and dark that it feels like stepping into a storybook. These contrasting scenes make every ride an adventure, with something new and beautiful around each bend. If you ride in the spring, you'll see the forest waking up from its winter slumber. Flowers bloom in a burst of color, and birds return from their winter travels to sing in the trees. In the summer, the trails are shaded by thick green leaves, making it the perfect time to go on long rides without getting too hot. Fall brings a golden glow as the leaves turn shades of red, orange, and yellow, carpeting the trails in a blanket of color. And if you're brave enough to bike in the winter, you'll find the forest quiet and covered in a layer of snow, where the only sounds are the crunch of your tires and the occasional hoot of an owl.

For those who like a bit of a challenge, the Black Forest also has trails designed for mountain biking. These paths are narrow, winding through rough terrain that tests your balance and skill. You might ride over roots that stick out from the ground, splash through shallow streams, or take sharp turns that keep you on your toes. Mountain biking in the Black Forest is a test of strength and courage, but it's also an incredible way to feel the thrill of adventure. One of the most popular mountain biking trails is the *Baden-Baden to Freudenstadt* route. It's long and demanding, but it takes you through some of the most untouched parts of the forest, where you might see wildlife like foxes or even a lynx if you're lucky.

Even on the quieter paths, there are plenty of moments that make biking in the Black Forest special. You might come across a small wooden bridge that crosses a clear, babbling brook. Stopping for a moment to listen to the water and look at the smooth stones underneath feels like finding a hidden treasure. There are also many trails that lead past waterfalls, such as the *Triberg Waterfalls*, which are among the highest in Germany. Hearing the roar of water and feeling the mist on your face as you approach is an experience you won't soon forget. Many bikers stop here to take photos or just sit and enjoy the natural beauty before continuing on their way.

If you're biking with friends or family, the experience becomes even more fun. You can race each other up small hills, share snacks while taking a break, and laugh at silly things that happen along the way, like trying to ride past a curious goat that's standing right in the middle of the path. And even when you're on your own, there's a special kind of peace that comes from riding through the forest, with only the sound of your bike and the rustle of leaves for company. The forest seems to whisper secrets to those who take the time to listen, and as you pedal through, you might find yourself thinking about all the people who have ridden those same trails before you, from ancient travelers on horseback to kids on bikes just like yours.

Safety is important when biking in the Black Forest, especially on longer or more challenging trails. Riders are encouraged to wear helmets and carry water, maps, and basic repair tools in case of a flat tire or loose chain. Fortunately, many trails are well-marked, with signs that point the way to nearby villages or popular landmarks. There are also plenty of places to stop and rest, with picnic areas where you can take a break and enjoy a packed lunch surrounded by the sounds and sights of the forest.

One of the most interesting things you might learn while biking through the Black Forest is how the trails were first made. Long ago, many of these paths were used by woodcutters and traders who carried goods between villages. Over time, they became part of the network of trails that now attract bikers from all over the world. It's amazing to think that the path you're riding on was once traveled by people who depended on it for their livelihood. This history adds another layer of wonder to every turn of the pedals.

Biking in the Black Forest is not just about the ride; it's about the feeling of being connected to nature and to the stories that have been passed down for generations. It's about seeing the way the sunlight filters through the branches and hearing the distant hum of village life blending with the sounds of the forest. It's about stopping to watch a rabbit dart across your path or taking a moment to look out at a valley that stretches far beyond where your eyes can see. Whether you're racing down a hill, exploring a new trail, or just coasting along at your own pace, biking in the Black Forest is an experience that fills your heart with a sense of wonder and leaves you with memories of a place that feels like it was made for adventure.

Chapter 18: The Forest's Biggest Festivals and Celebrations

The Black Forest, with its deep green trees, rolling hills, and charming villages, is not only a place of natural wonder but also a hub for some of the most vibrant festivals and celebrations in Germany. These festivals are a blend of age-old traditions, local folklore, music, dancing, and delicious food, making them an unforgettable experience for anyone who takes part. The people of the Black Forest take great pride in their customs, and every year they gather to celebrate with joy, turning their towns and villages into places filled with laughter, color, and a sense of community.

One of the biggest and most beloved festivals in the Black Forest is the *Fasnacht*, or the Carnival season. This festival, which takes place in late winter before Lent begins, is a time when the towns come alive with parades, costumes, and masks that are both fun and a bit spooky. The streets are filled with people wearing traditional masks carved from wood, each one representing a different character or spirit from local folklore. Some masks are funny, with wide, grinning mouths and big, round eyes, while others are fierce, with sharp teeth and wild hair, meant to chase away the last cold spirits of winter. Music plays loudly as marching bands, dressed in bright costumes, lead the parades through the cobblestone streets. Drums beat a fast, exciting rhythm, and trumpets blare, adding to the festival's electric atmosphere.

The *Fasnacht* is more than just a party; it has deep roots in the history and beliefs of the people who live there. Long ago, villagers believed that winter was controlled by dark, cold spirits that needed to be scared away so that spring could come. The masks and costumes worn during *Fasnacht* were meant to frighten these spirits and ensure that warmer, brighter days were on their way. Even today, as people dance and sing through the streets, you can feel the old traditions blending with the excitement of the present. Children love to join in, wearing their own fun costumes and chasing each other while adults throw sweets and confetti into the air.

Spring in the Black Forest brings another special celebration: the *Easter Markets*. These markets are set up in village squares, decorated with colorful flowers, painted eggs, and garlands made of twigs and blossoms. People gather to browse stalls that sell handmade crafts, traditional wooden toys, and freshly baked bread and pastries. One of the most delightful treats you might find at an Easter market is the *Osterfladen*, a sweet, fluffy cake that's often shared with friends and family. Musicians play soft tunes on violins and flutes, adding a cheerful soundtrack to the day as children take part in egg-painting workshops or go on Easter egg hunts through the village. The markets are a time for everyone to come together, share stories, and enjoy the start of warmer weather.

Summer in the Black Forest is filled with festivals that celebrate the beauty of the land and the hard work of its people. One of the most spectacular summer events is the *Schwarzwaldklänge*, or the Sounds of the Black Forest festival. This is when musicians from across the region gather to play traditional folk music using instruments like the accordion, the zither, and wooden flutes. The festival takes place outdoors, with stages set up in meadows and on hillsides surrounded by trees. People spread out blankets, bring picnic baskets, and spend the day enjoying the music and the sunshine. Dancers in traditional *Trachten* costumes, with their embroidered vests, skirts, and feathered hats, spin and twirl in rhythm with the music, their steps a dance passed down through generations.

One of the highlights of the *Schwarzwaldklänge* is the yodeling competition. Yodeling is an old way of singing that jumps quickly between high and low notes, creating a sound that echoes across the hills. The best yodelers can make their voices carry for miles, and during the festival, their songs can be heard ringing through the forest.

Children try their hand at yodeling too, laughing as their voices crack or squeak in surprise. It's a joyful event that makes everyone feel connected, not just to each other but to the land around them.

As summer moves into fall, the Black Forest holds another beloved tradition: the *Harvest Festival*. This festival celebrates the end of the farming season and the gathering of crops. Villages are decorated with straw bales, pumpkins, and sheaves of wheat, and everyone comes out to take part in the celebration. The festival starts with a parade led by farmers driving old-fashioned tractors decorated with flowers and ribbons. Behind them, wagons piled high with apples, cabbages, and other harvest goodies roll slowly through the streets. People wave and cheer, happy for the abundance the season has brought.

Food is a big part of the *Harvest Festival*, and there are tables overflowing with traditional dishes. You might find *Bratwurst* sizzling on grills, steaming bowls of potato soup, and big pretzels sprinkled with salt. For dessert, there's always a generous slice of Black Forest cake, made with layers of chocolate sponge, cherries, and whipped cream. Local cider and apple juice, made from the region's own orchards, are poured into cups and shared around. At the center of the festival, a large maypole is raised, and people gather to dance around it, holding hands and moving in a circle as music fills the air.

Winter in the Black Forest is a time of warmth and magic, especially when the *Christmas Markets* come to life. These markets are famous for their twinkling lights, wooden stalls, and the smell of roasted chestnuts and spiced gingerbread. Each village has its own unique take on the Christmas market, but all of them share the same cozy, festive spirit. Vendors sell handmade ornaments carved from wood, delicate glass baubles, and knitted scarves and gloves to keep warm during the chilly evenings. One of the most special treats is the *Stollen*, a traditional holiday bread filled with dried fruits and dusted with powdered sugar. Children gather around storytellers who share tales of Saint Nicholas and his trusty sidekick, the kind but mysterious *Pelznickel*, who is said to visit children during the holiday season.

Music plays an important role in the Christmas celebrations, with carolers singing in the streets and church choirs performing beautiful, harmonious songs that echo in the cold night air. There are often small performances of traditional nativity plays, complete with costumes and wooden cribs, that tell the story of the first Christmas. In some towns, a procession of people dressed as angels, shepherds, and wise men walks through the village, their lanterns casting a golden glow against the dark sky. Snow sometimes falls during these processions, adding an extra touch of magic to the scene.

Another winter tradition in the Black Forest is the *Feuerzangenbowle* celebration. This event is named after a special drink made by placing a sugarloaf soaked in rum over a bowl of mulled wine and then setting it on fire. The sugar caramelizes and drips into the wine, creating a sweet, warm drink that's perfect for cold nights. People gather around to watch the flames dance and share stories, their faces lit up by the fire's glow. This tradition is especially popular among adults, but children enjoy watching the spectacle and sipping hot chocolate while they listen to the cheerful chatter.

No matter the season, the festivals and celebrations of the Black Forest are filled with joy, tradition, and a deep connection to the land and its people. These events bring families, friends, and even visitors from far away together, creating memories that last a lifetime. Whether it's the sight of colorful masks at *Fasnacht*, the sound of yodeling at a summer festival, or the taste of warm gingerbread at a Christmas market, the celebrations of the Black Forest capture the spirit of a place that's as alive with history as it is with beauty.

Chapter 19: Black Forest Adventures in Winter

Winter in the Black Forest is like stepping into a scene from a storybook. When the first snowfall covers the forest, everything transforms into a magical winter wonderland. The tall pines and ancient oaks become wrapped in thick layers of snow, their branches bending gently under the weight. Paths that were once alive with the sound of crunching leaves in the fall turn silent, muffled by the soft, white blanket. The air is crisp and cold, tinged with the fresh, earthy scent of pine and the hint of wood smoke drifting from nearby village chimneys. For those looking for adventure, winter in the Black Forest offers a mix of thrilling activities, cozy moments, and a touch of magic that makes this time of year unforgettable.

One of the most exciting adventures in the Black Forest during winter is skiing. The region is home to some of the best ski slopes in Germany, with options for beginners and seasoned skiers alike. The *Feldberg Mountain*, the highest peak in the Black Forest, is a popular destination for skiing and snowboarding. With well-maintained trails and lifts that carry skiers to the top, it's the perfect spot for racing down the snowy slopes and feeling the cool wind rush past. For those new to skiing, friendly instructors are available to help with lessons, making it a great place for kids and families to learn together. After a day on the slopes, skiers often head to cozy mountain lodges to warm up by a roaring fire, sipping hot chocolate or mulled cider.

Cross-country skiing is another popular winter activity in the Black Forest. Unlike downhill skiing, cross-country skiing takes you through the quieter, more hidden parts of the forest. Gliding over smooth, snowy paths, skiers can explore trails that wind between trees, past frozen lakes, and over gentle hills. It's a peaceful experience where the only sound might be the swish of skis moving through the snow and the occasional call of a bird or rustle of a deer in the distance. The Black Forest boasts a vast network of cross-country trails that vary in difficulty, so there's always something new to discover. Some routes lead to lookouts that offer breathtaking views of snow-covered valleys and villages with their rooftops dusted in white.

For those who love winter adventures but prefer something a little slower, snowshoeing is a perfect option. Snowshoes make it easier to walk over deep snow, allowing explorers to venture into areas that might be difficult to reach otherwise. Hiking through the woods on snowshoes is like taking a trip back in time, as the quiet paths feel untouched and serene. Adventurers might come across animal tracks left in the snow—like the tiny, delicate footprints of a fox or the large, heavy prints of a wild boar. Snowshoeing in the Black Forest is often accompanied by guided tours, where local guides share stories about the forest's history and its animals, weaving tales that bring the snowy landscape to life.

Sledding is another winter favorite that brings out the kid in everyone. The Black Forest is full of perfect sledding hills, some gentle and easy for little ones and others steep and fast for those who crave excitement. Families gather on these snowy slopes, bundled up in warm coats, scarves, and hats. The laughter and shouts of excitement as sleds race down the hill fill the chilly air. One of the most popular spots for sledding is the *Sausenburg Castle* area, where an old stone ruin adds a touch of mystery and adventure to the day. After sledding, kids and parents often build snowmen or have playful snowball fights, creating fun memories to last long after the snow has melted.

When it comes to winter activities, the Black Forest also offers the unique experience of ice skating on natural lakes. When the weather is cold enough and the lakes freeze over, they become sparkling ice rinks surrounded by snow-covered trees. Skating on a frozen lake feels different from an indoor rink; there's a sense of freedom and adventure as you glide across the clear ice, the wind nipping at your cheeks. One of the most well-known places for ice skating is *Lake Titisee*, a popular spot that turns into a winter paradise. The lake is large enough for skaters to have plenty of space to twirl, race, or practice their skating tricks. For those who prefer to watch, there's often hot drinks and warm snacks available from nearby stalls, making it a cozy outing even for non-skaters.

Winter in the Black Forest wouldn't be complete without its magical Christmas markets. These markets are known all over the world for their charm and festive spirit. Each village and town has its own version, but all share twinkling lights, the smell of roasted chestnuts, and the joyful sounds of carolers singing familiar holiday songs. Stalls made of wood are decorated with garlands and sell handmade crafts, ornaments, and warm woolen clothes. Visitors can try traditional treats like *Lebkuchen* (a spiced gingerbread), or warm up with a steaming cup of *Glühwein* (a spiced, hot wine). Children especially love seeing the life-sized nativity scenes and twinkling lights strung from trees, creating a scene that feels like it's right out of a Christmas story.

Evenings in the Black Forest during winter are cozy and peaceful. Many visitors enjoy a slow walk through a village, where the streets are lined with lanterns casting a warm glow over the snow. Families might stay in traditional timber-framed guesthouses with wood-burning fireplaces that crackle and fill the rooms with a comforting heat. Storytelling nights are popular in the winter, where people gather to listen to tales of forest spirits and ancient legends. Wrapped in blankets, sipping hot cocoa, and watching the firelight dance on the walls, it's easy to imagine the myths coming to life outside in the snowy forest.

A particularly unique adventure in the Black Forest during winter is the guided night hikes. With lanterns or headlamps lighting the way, hikers set off into the moonlit forest, their breath forming clouds in the cold night air. The forest looks completely different at night, with shadows stretching out from the trees and the sky dotted with stars.

Sometimes, the guides share stories about the constellations or the local myths connected to the night sky. The quiet of the forest at night, interrupted only by the crunch of snow underfoot and the occasional hoot of an owl, makes these hikes feel both thrilling and peaceful.

For visitors looking for a more relaxing winter experience, the Black Forest is also famous for its thermal baths. After a day of skiing, snowshoeing, or exploring, soaking in warm, mineral-rich water is a perfect way to unwind. The thermal baths are said to have healing properties, and many are surrounded by scenic views of the forest. Some of the most well-known thermal spas can be found in *Baden-Baden*, a town famous for its luxurious baths that have been enjoyed since Roman times. Here, visitors can enjoy indoor and outdoor pools, surrounded by the beauty of the forest while the steam rises into the chilly winter air.

Winter in the Black Forest is full of surprises, from the joy of racing down snowy hills to the quiet magic of walking through a village aglow with Christmas lights. It's a time when the forest feels alive with traditions and stories, and the simple pleasures of the season—like warming your hands around a hot drink or listening to carolers sing—become moments to treasure. Whether you come for the adventure of skiing, the fun of sledding, the wonder of Christmas markets, or the peaceful beauty of the snow-covered landscape, winter in the Black Forest is an experience filled with wonder and joy. The forest, so full of life in the warmer months, shows a quieter, yet equally enchanting, side when it's blanketed in snow, inviting everyone who visits to make memories that sparkle like frost in the morning sun.

Chapter 20: Protecting the Forest and Its Future

The Black Forest is one of the most beautiful and enchanting places in the world, known for its dense woodlands, rolling hills, and the wildlife that calls it home. This forest has been around for thousands of years and has a rich history filled with legends, folklore, and the traditions of the people who have lived there for generations. But just like any magical place on Earth, the Black Forest needs to be protected to ensure that it remains healthy and vibrant for years to come. This means that everyone, from scientists and forest rangers to families and children who live nearby or visit, has an important part to play in protecting the forest and caring for its future.

The first step in protecting the Black Forest is understanding why it's so special. The forest is home to thousands of plant and animal species, many of which are unique to this region. It provides a habitat for wild boars, deer, foxes, owls, and even lynxes, which are rare and beautiful wild cats that have recently made a return to the area. The trees themselves, like tall pines, firs, and oaks, create a canopy that helps clean the air and provide oxygen, making the forest an essential part of the Earth's ecosystem. It's not just the plants and animals that rely on the forest—people do too. The Black Forest is a place for hiking, biking, and exploring, which brings joy to visitors and locals alike. It also provides wood and other natural resources that have been used for centuries to make furniture, build homes, and create traditional crafts.

One of the biggest challenges in protecting the Black Forest is the impact of human activity. In the past, the forest was heavily logged to provide wood for building and fuel. While some logging is necessary and can be done in a way that keeps the forest healthy, cutting down too many trees or doing so without careful planning can harm the environment. Deforestation not only destroys the homes of animals but also weakens the soil, making it easier for rain to wash away the nutrients that plants need to grow. Today, forest management teams are working hard to make sure that the trees are cut down in a way that allows the forest to regenerate. This means that when trees are taken for wood, new trees are planted to take their place, creating a sustainable cycle that supports both people and nature.

Pollution is another concern for the Black Forest. Car exhaust, factory smoke, and other forms of pollution can damage the trees and the plants on the forest floor. Acid rain, which is caused by pollution mixing with rainwater, can be especially harmful as it weakens the trees and makes them more vulnerable to disease and pests. Scientists and environmentalists are working on solutions to these problems, such as finding cleaner ways to power factories and encouraging people to use eco-friendly transportation like bicycles or electric cars. By reducing pollution, the forest can stay healthy, and the air we breathe can remain fresh and clean.

Climate change is another challenge that affects the Black Forest. Warmer temperatures and changing weather patterns can lead to problems such as droughts, where the forest doesn't get enough rain. This makes it harder for trees to grow and thrive, and it can even increase the risk of forest fires. While wildfires are sometimes a natural part of a forest's lifecycle, helping to clear old or diseased trees and make room for new growth, uncontrolled wildfires can be devastating. They can destroy huge areas of forest in a very short time and displace the animals that live there. To help combat the effects of climate change, local governments and forest conservation groups have started programs that focus on reforestation, which means planting trees in areas where they've been lost, and studying the types of trees that are more resilient to changes in climate.

Education plays a huge role in protecting the Black Forest for future generations. Schools and community groups often organize field trips and outdoor lessons that teach children about the importance of the forest and how they can help take care of it. These lessons might include learning how to identify different types of trees, understanding which animals are endangered, and finding out why it's important to pick up litter and keep trails clean. Kids can also learn about the small actions they can take to protect the forest, such as recycling, using less water, and supporting eco-friendly products. These lessons help build a lifelong appreciation for nature and show young people that they have the power to make a difference.

Forest rangers and park wardens play a big part in protecting the Black Forest. Their job is to watch over the forest, making sure that visitors follow the rules that keep the environment safe. They check for signs of illegal logging or poaching, which is the hunting of animals that are protected by law. They also work to prevent forest fires by creating firebreaks, which are gaps in vegetation that stop a fire from spreading too far. When winter arrives and the forest is covered in snow, rangers make sure that people using the forest for activities like skiing or snowshoeing stay on the designated paths so that the delicate plants and wildlife underneath the snow are not harmed. Rangers also help injured animals they come across and take care of them until they can return safely to the wild.

One of the most interesting projects aimed at protecting the Black Forest involves the use of modern technology. Drones and satellites are now being used to monitor the health of the forest from above. With these tools, scientists can get a clear picture of how many trees are in an area, check for signs of disease or damage, and track the movement of animals. This bird's-eye view helps experts plan how to care for the forest and take action before problems become too big. For example, if a certain part of the forest is drying out or showing signs of stress due to climate change, conservation teams can step in to water the area or plant more drought-resistant trees.

Local farmers also play a role in protecting the Black Forest. Many farmers who live on the edges of the forest work with conservation groups to use sustainable farming practices. This means they grow crops or raise animals in a way that doesn't harm the forest or the wildlife. For example, they might create hedgerows and wildflower borders that provide food and shelter for birds and insects. Farmers can also avoid using harmful pesticides that could run off into the streams and rivers that flow through the forest, keeping the water clean for fish and other aquatic animals.

Communities that live in and around the Black Forest also have their traditions that help protect their homeland. These traditions include planting trees during festivals or celebrating the forest with folk songs that remind people of the importance of nature. Craftsmen who create the famous Black Forest cuckoo clocks often use wood that comes from sustainable sources, ensuring that their art does not contribute to deforestation. Even the recipes for traditional dishes like Black Forest cake or sausages often include local ingredients, which supports farmers and reduces the need for long-distance transportation that adds to pollution.

Tourism is a big part of life in the Black Forest, but it's important to make sure that visitors respect the land. Eco-tourism programs encourage visitors to explore the forest in a way that doesn't harm the environment. This means staying on marked paths, not picking wildflowers, and making sure to leave no trash behind. Visitors are also encouraged to support local businesses that use environmentally friendly practices, such as guesthouses that run on renewable energy or restaurants that source their food locally. Guided nature tours led by knowledgeable guides teach visitors about the delicate balance of life in the forest, from the way fungi break down fallen leaves to how certain birds help spread seeds that grow into new trees.

Protecting the future of the Black Forest also involves making sure that endangered animals have a safe place to live. Conservation groups work to protect the habitats of animals like the capercaillie, a large, rare bird with beautiful feathers that is known for its unique dance and song. Efforts to save these animals include creating quiet zones where people cannot go during certain times of the year, especially when animals are nesting or raising their young. By giving wildlife space to live without being disturbed, the forest remains a thriving place where all kinds of creatures can continue to exist.

In the end, protecting the Black Forest and ensuring its future is about creating a balance between human needs and nature. It means remembering that while the forest can provide wood, food, and fun adventures, it is also a home to countless living things and a vital part of the Earth's ecosystem. People of all ages can help in their own way, whether by learning about the forest, teaching others, supporting conservation efforts, or simply treating the land with kindness and respect when they visit. The more people who understand the importance of the Black Forest, the better chance it has to remain a place full of life, beauty, and magic for generations to come.

Epilogue

As our journey through the Black Forest comes to an end, I hope you feel like you've uncovered some of its many wonders. From the magical stories that have been told for generations to the animals that sneak through the trees at night, the Black Forest is a place full of adventure and mystery. You now know about the ancient castles that stand proudly on the hills, the cuckoo clocks that tell time with a song, and the tasty Black Forest cakes that make mouths water around the world.

But beyond all the legends and tales, the Black Forest is a reminder of the incredible power and beauty of nature. It's a place where old and new come together, where people and wildlife share the same space, and where every tree and river has a story to tell. Whether you ever visit in person or dream about it from afar, the Black Forest will always be a place where imagination can run wild.

Now that you've explored its secrets, you're ready to become a storyteller of the Black Forest yourself. Share what you've learned, tell your friends about the hidden caves and ancient myths, and keep the magic alive by protecting nature wherever you go.

The Black Forest will always be there, waiting for the next curious mind and brave heart. And who knows? Maybe one day you'll step foot on its winding trails and discover a story of your own. Until then, keep exploring, keep wondering, and remember: the world is full of places just as mysterious and amazing, waiting for you to find them.

The adventure never truly ends—it's only the beginning.

The End.

Milton Keynes UK
Ingram Content Group UK Ltd.
UKHW030853151124
451262UK00001B/199